When I See Her Smile

Bears in Love Series

Book Two

PA Vachon

Dedication

For my husband. As always, you are my light, my love, my strength, and my home. For Angel. You are my soul sister and sharer of our one brain. To all who have stood with me and helped me along the way on this amazing journey, you are all rock stars! And to the ladies of P.A.'s BearsandBabes, you are the best team ever. Thank you for all of your love and support. It means everything!!! Smooches…

Praise for Mated to the Grizzly…

PA Vachon's debut novel is a paranormal treasure! Great characters, plenty of action that will keep your heart rate up and sizzling hot heat, this book was perfectly paced ~ Marie Brown Blogger/Reviewer ~ Marie's Tempting Reads

This is the first book by this author and was so well written I could see and hear every fight and sex scene. ~ Terri O'Connell ~ Reader

Really good story, thoroughly enjoyed it. I love Lauren and Ian and their relationship, which was intense and oh so hot. I can't wait to read the next book in this series and more by this author~ Annamarie Gardner ~ Reader

Prologue

Twelve years earlier…

I watched as the tail lights on my mom's car got further and further away, disappearing down the road at a high rate of speed. I wanted to race after her and get her to stop the car and take me home. She didn't stop though. She kept driving. I wouldn't cry, because nine year olds didn't cry. Especially not nine year old polar bear shifters. I walked up to the door and knocked. I waited several minutes, and then a harried looking older woman answered the door, looking me up and down and letting me in the door.

"Well, what do we have here?" she asked with a kind smile.

"My name is Trevor. Trevor Mannus," I supplied. "I'm nine years old, and my mom just left me here."

1

The kind eyed lady ushered me further into the house and closed the door.

"Well, Trevor, that's ok," she said. "We'll figure that all out tomorrow. Are you hungry?"

"No, ma'am," I answered, but my stomach chose that moment to grumble and make me into a liar. She gave me a small, smiling laugh, saying, "My name is Mrs. Robins. Let's get you something to eat."

That first night, I ate and slept, and the next day, children's services came to ask me some questions. I answered them as best as I could. I was with Mrs. Robins for six months, she was the nice older lady who had taken me in when my mom abandoned me. She got really sick, and I ended up in a group home. It was the worst two weeks of my life.

During those two weeks that I was in the group home Mrs. Robins died. She had pneumonia and she didn't get it treated quickly enough. It killed her. While at the group home, I struggled to keep my bear under control. I knew that was why my mom left me that night. She couldn't handle my bear. She had never told me about my dad, so all I knew was that they were mates, mom got pregnant, and he disappeared for good.

After two weeks at the group home, I had gotten tired of being the punching bag for the bigger older kids. I ran. Two years later, I ended up outside Fall City, Washington, hungry, cold, and alone. That's when Marcus found me, digging through a garbage can, looking for something edible to tide me over.

"Kid, I don't think you're gonna want to eat anything you find in there," he said to me that first night.

"Maybe not, but it's better than starving," I replied. I had been in Seattle, barely surviving, for two years. I was now almost twelve. My polar bear was unpredictable. I knew Marcus was a bear of some sort. I could smell that on him, but I wasn't sure what kind.

"Well, you can come home with me," Marcus said. "I've got food and a warm place for you to stay. I also have a place you can shift."

I thought about it for a bit. Was this guy a weirdo who liked boys or just a kind man who really wanted to help? I hoped I wasn't making the wrong choice.

"I would appreciate that, sir," I told him.

"Well, come on then," Marcus laughingly said. "Food waits for no man."

It took almost an hour for him to get my name from me. By the time I went to bed, I had a pseudo sister and brother, Regan and Ian. They would also become my best friends and fellow Secret Keepers.

Almost ten years later, Ian would meet his mate Lauren and fall head over heels. It wouldn't be all sunshine and roses though. Not even close. Ian met Lauren during a mission, and she was kidnapped by

Hatchet, a maniac with an axe to grind and his own agenda. During that time, I would meet a woman, Janet, who I thought was my mate (young adult male hormones were in full control at this point), and she would almost end me. She bruised me for a while. But I wasn't dead yet.

This is the story of how I found my heart and soul. This is the story of how I gained everything. It isn't an instant happily ever after though, so sit back and read about how one woman's smile would heal all my open wounds.

Chapter 1

~Trevor~

I didn't think I would ever meet my one, my soul mate. Those bitches that control Fate have always laughed at me and jerked my life strings to and fro, from being raised in an orphanage because my mom couldn't handle a young shifter male without my father until I was found by Marcus close to my twelfth birthday to thinking I had found my mate as a young adult. I blame my raging hormones for that shit show. I had just turned nineteen, and she was beautiful, but that beauty hid grasping, greedy, evil thoughts and deeds behind her facade. She was almost the death of me, and when I found out she had been sent to infiltrate our clan and spy for Hatchet when Ian and Lauren were just mated, I lost what little hope I had forever. Almost two years later, the clan is still trying to mend from her deviousness. And I am still alone. I have my clan, who is like a family, but I don't have my one. I am starting to think I lost my chance. I was not prepared for what happened next. Not one little bit.

I was sent into Fall City, Washington, to get supplies for the week. While there, I visited The Roadhouse Restaurant and Inn, a small clapboard building that dated back to 1916, and that's when it happened. Instant hard-on and not just because she was beautiful, but because she was mine. She smiled at me as she walked up to my table to take my order, and my polar bear rushed to the surface. Yep, a polar in a grizzly clan. Not something you see everyday, but Marcus, the clan's leader and all around giant grizzly, is my pseudo-dad figure, and once you are in, that's it. Your clan, your family. I had to concentrate on holding my bear back. I got a whiff of her scent, like fresh snow and pine trees, and I had to grip the table sides to keep myself in my seat. My polar, and if I am honest, my human self, wanted to grab up this vision and take her away to keep her to myself.

"Hey, I'm Rebecca and I'll be your server," she said. "What can I get you today?" the vision in front of me asked.

"Ummm, uhh, a beer would be great," I stuttered out.

"What's your poison, handsome?" she laughingly inquired. "We have Bud, Miller, or we have some great microbrews."

"Bottle of Bud, please," I told her.

"You got it," she said. "Did you want anything to eat with that?"

"No thanks," I said.

She turned to get my beer, and I watched her ass as she walked away. And what an ass it was, just enough to hold onto and worship, but not so much that it was too large. I could imagine myself caressing and slapping that ass as we fucked.

■■■

~Rebecca~

I could feel my customer's eyes on my backside as I walked away, so I put a little extra wiggle into my walk. Let's face it, extra tips were nothing to sneer at. I had the bartender get me the bottle of Bud and returned to the table to deliver it.

"Here ya go, handsome," I said. "Can I get you anything else?"

"Your phone number would be nice," he playfully said, seeming to recover from his earlier starstruck immaturity.

"Sorry, no can do, sir," I said.

****

~Trevor~

She turned to go to the next customer when a giant hand was wrapped around her wrist in a light grip. She looked down at his hand and said,

"I'm gonna need you to let go, please."

"I just want to get to know you better, darling," Trevor was anxious to make sure she didn't get away without some way to contact her.

"Look... What's your name?" she asked.

"Trevor, I'm Trevor Mannus," was his reply.

"Look, Trevor, it's really busy right now, and I need to get back to work. Let me go, please," Rebecca huffed.

Trevor looked to where his hand encircled her wrist. "Oops, sorry. Can we meet up when you are off shift?" he asked.

"Maybe. I get off at ten tonight," she told him.

"I'll be here, beautiful," Trevor said, releasing her wrist to let her get back to work.

"Okay, then," she turned to go again, heading for her next table. When she saw who was sitting there, she wished she had just stayed with Trevor.

It was her ex, Alan. He had been in the last several times she had worked, harassing her to no end. It was getting really old. He thought he wanted her back, but that wasn't gonna happen. It's not every day you walk into your shared apartment to see your supposed best friend bent over your couch with your boyfriend's dick buried in his ass. Yep, apparently Alan liked both teams. He just forgot to mention it to Rebecca.

"Alan, what can I get for you?" she shuddered slightly.

"I want you back, babe," he slurred. Great, he was already lit.

****

~Rebecca~

"Not happening, Alan," I gritted out.

I walked away to give myself some time before I did something to lose my job. I walked towards the hallway where the restrooms were to cool off. I leaned my forehead against the side wall and took two deep breaths. I felt more than saw a very large, warm presence. I knew it wasn't Alan; he was only a couple inches taller than my 5'5". This person was at least a foot taller than me. I turned my head without leaving the wall. It was Trevor. I closed my eyes again and groaned.

"Darling, you look frustrated," Trevor stated as he put his large warm hand on my shoulder. "Is there anything I can do to help?"

"Unless you can make someone disappear without a trace, then no," I muttered.

"Babe, for you, I could do anything," he replied.

I looked up into eyes the color of the sky on a stormy day, such a dark gray that they were almost black. His hair was a dark chocolate brown, like my favorite candy bar. And he was tall, so tall.

"Jesus, how tall are you?" rushed out of my mouth before I could pull it back.

He husked out a laugh, sounding like he didn't laugh often.

"6'4", babe," he said.

He gently pulled me into him and hugged me to his front. I was in heaven. It was amazing. I felt safe, so I let my eyes close as I savored the moment, knowing that I would have to let go sooner rather than later. But a girl needs comfort when confronted by her cheating ex.

"Hey, let her go, Neanderthal," I heard shouted from the entrance to the hallway. Shit, it was Alan. I tried to pull Trevor closer, to no avail. He leaned away from me and looked at Alan.

"Dude, we are having a private conversation," Trevor said. "You need to get off."

"That's my girlfriend, dick. Let her go," Alan ordered.

"Alan, I am not your girlfriend. You lost the right to call me that when your dick was stuck up Jerry's ass,"

I spewed venomously at him as I glared. If looks could kill, he would have died right then.

Trevor looked back down at me and searched my eyes. He then turned and angled his body in front of mine, out of protection or so it seemed.

"I'm only going to ask you once," Trevor growled. "Then we are gonna have a problem."

Alan made to move closer, and I heard what sounded like an animal's growl come from Trevor. Alan stopped and then went to take another step.

"Not a good idea, dude," I told him from behind Trevor. I could feel the pent up rage radiating off of Trevor like waves of energy. It was otherworldly. It didn't concern me. I actually wanted to shift closer to his back to feel more of the magnetic power I could sense.

Alan took another step towards us. He was now only about two feet from Trevor. Trevor's hands

15

fisted, and I heard another growl come from deep within him. He blocked more of me with his large body. Oddly, I wasn't freaking out. I felt safe, protected.

Alan advanced again, and that's when Trevor threw the first and last punch. Alan hit the ground like a bag of bricks. I stared down at my ex, not really happy that he was out, but relieved that I wouldn't have to deal with him anymore.

"Come on, babe," Trevor soothed. "Let's get out of here, yeah?"

I nodded my head in agreement. We walked back to the bar, where I told the bartender and our manager that I wasn't feeling well and I needed to go for the rest of the night. I was waved off and told to feel better.

We walked out the front of the building and headed towards the parking lot. My beater was parked at the back of the lot. I started to head towards my car when Trevor stopped me by gently taking my hand.

"Rebecca, wait," he began. "I want you to come home with me, please."

I looked at him like he had grown an extra head. "I can't go home with you, crazy man."

Trevor chuckled. "I meant come home with me to my family compound. I want to keep you safe. That guy doesn't seem the type to give up."

"You're right, he's not, but I'll be fine. He won't do anything else tonight. I doubt he'll be up for much of anything after that hit. I can't go home with you," I told him earnestly.

"Babe, you can stay with my best friend, Ian, and his wife, Lauren. They won't mind," he said.

"I can't stay with your friends either. What is your damage?" I scoffed.

"Just, please, come home with me," he leaned in and captured my lips in a searing kiss. My knees weakened, as did my resolve. Trevor pulled away from my lips, causing me to whimper. He looked into my eyes, gently holding me in his large grip, like a fragile piece of glass.

"Okay, but only for tonight," I acquiesced.

Trevor broke out into a shit eating grin, larger than any I had ever seen. As we walked hand in hand, he led me to a motorcycle sitting close to the front of the parking lot. I stopped. "Ummm, Trevor, I can't ride a motorcycle," I started to say.

"It's all good, babe. I have an extra helmet." Trevor stopped at the side of his bike that was black as sin and probably just as dangerous. He removed the helmets strapped to the back.

"Here, babe. This one is for you." Trevor tried to hand me the smaller of the two helmets. I looked at him, askance.

"I'm not sure about this, Trevor," I began again. "I've never ridden a motorcycle before and my granny always said 'Rebecca Ann, you stay off those devil machines.' "

"Rebecca Ann, huh?" Trevor asked. "I like it, babe."

"Of what I just said, that is what you zero in on, my full name," she said. "Really?"

"Baby, no worries. If you're lucky, it will be the second best thing between your legs tonight, beautiful," he teasingly said as he straddled the seat of his bike, buckling his helmet into place. "Come on, babe. We haven't got all night." He grinned over at me as he patted the seat behind him.

19

I huffed out a breath and put the helmet on. I wasn't afraid, just cautious. Oh who was I kidding, I was totally scared out of my mind and turned on maybe a little too much. I wanted to stay the night with Trevor, but I didn't want to be another notch on his bedpost. Of course, I didn't know him well enough to make those judgements. I only had to go on my previous experience. None of it was very good. Alan cheated on me with Jerry. Before that it was Ben and Lila, another one of my so called friends. But I think the most consistent and well rehearsed of all the crappy things people have ever done or said belongs to my mother, Lisa. My mother, who should have been my greatest protector and champion, was actually the worst offender of all. It started when I was a pre-teen with digs about the baby fat, which I couldn't seem to lose, and about my hair, which never met a brush that could tame it. In my teen years, it got worse. While I wasn't exactly skinny, my curves were pretty dangerous, and that was like a threat to my mother. In retrospect, I should have caught on when she started flirting with my teenage boyfriends. I moved out as soon as the ink was dry on my diploma. Unfortunately, I moved in with Lila. She and Ben were humping behind my back for almost six months before I caught on. Humiliating, to say the least. The coffee cups that were left in our shared apartment walls cost me my half of the security deposit. Then I moved on to Alan, who is still apparently in the closet.

"Babe, you gotta get on the bike," Trevor laughingly said, "or we can't go anywhere."

"Ha, ha, Trevor," I said as I took the helmet from him with a slight glare.

I strapped the helmet on and awkwardly mounted the bike, gripping Trevor's shoulders once I was settled on the seat.

"Baby, you are gonna need to hold on to my waist or you're gonna go flying off the back of my bike," he told me, laughing as he pulled me closer to his back with his hand on my hip, a hand that burned like fire.

21

His large hands felt so good, I wanted to purr and arch into his back like a cat in heat. Instead, I scooched closer to him. I breathed in his manly scent. It was like forest and moonlight. Pine and a touch of magic.

"Stop sniffing me, darling, or we won't make it to my house," he gruffly said.

"Sorry, but you smell so good," I said. Oh lord, my mouth was gonna get me in so much trouble. I was sure I was beet red. Good thing it was dark. Trevor wouldn't be able to see my rosy red cheeks.

Trevor grinned over his shoulder at me. "You smell amazing too, baby. Wait til I get you to my house."

"Trevor, we are not staying together. You said I could stay with your friends and *THAT* is what I agreed to," I angrily hissed.

"I know, babe. I'm just yanking your chain." Trevor gunned the engine of the bike, and we were off with a squeal of tires on asphalt.

I let out a very unladylike "Oh, Shit!" as I gripped Trevor's waist ever tighter. I would never tell him, but this was the best thing I had ever done. We sped through the night, the wind whipping and the trees flying by at top speed. We came to a closed gate that was attached to a large stone wall. Trevor stopped and pushed a button on the handlebars of his bike, and the gate slowly swung open to reveal a very large compound with several flood lights around the perimeter.

I stared in awe, wondering why they needed so much security. But I didn't voice my concerns. Instead, we pulled up to a small one story cabin with a large front porch.

"Is this your friend's place?" I asked Trevor, looking at the darkened windows pensively.

"No, baby. This is my cabin," Trevor said. "I just need to check on some things before we go over to Ian's." Trevor pointed across the large parking area to another darkened cabin.

While Trevor walked toward the front porch, I thought about what I really wanted. Did I want to stay with his friends? Did I really want to stay away from him? I knew the answers to both the questions. I took a deep fortifying breath and then I said,

"Trevor, I don't want to bother your friends this late. It looks like they are sleeping." I nervously watched as he grinned down at me.

"They won't mind, babe. Come on, I'll give you the nickel tour, and then we can head across the compound," Trevor told me.

Trevor opened the front door to reveal my dream. The cabin was decorated with rustic log furniture. I loved the outdoorsy feel of the living room. To one

24

side, the couch sat with cushy pillows and throw blankets, the extra fuzzy ones. I loved those on cold nights. Across from the couch was a large open hearth fireplace with a stack of logs ready to burn. It was a chilly night. I thought that maybe I should just stay with Trevor so that we didn't bother his friends, so I stated as much. Trevor's response was to eye me up and down, twice, as if he was gauging my honesty.

I walked towards him. I stopped within a hair's breadth of his body. I looked up into his eyes, riveted in place by the look of dominance that I saw there. I took a shaky breath and said,

"Trevor, I don't want to bother Ian and his wife. I want to stay here. With you, if the offer is still open. I can sleep on your couch."

"You aren't sleeping on the couch if you are staying here, babe. Not happening," Trevor growled.

He pulled me to him and we collided. I tilted my head, and Trevor bent towards me. This kiss was not as all-consuming as the first, but it still left a mark on my soul. I had never had a kiss as sweet. Before, it was always this wet, messy tangle that was more dead fish than sexy. Alan was not the best lover. Of course, now I knew why, but at the time, it was self-esteem killing. He had always blamed my looks and personality for his ineptness. Trevor kissed me with reverence, like he wasn't sure if I was real. I gasped into his mouth as he deepened our kiss. It was like chocolate and cinnamon combined together to create this perfect moment of bliss.

Trevor pulled back, and I smiled shyly up at him with a blush. I was never this forward. I was not that girl who slept with any Tom, Dick, or cock, but there was something about Trevor that lent itself to safety and comfort. I needed him like an alcoholic needs a drink or an addict needs their next fix.

"I love when you smile. That was the first thing I noticed about you at the pub," Trevor admitted.

Trevor then led me down the hall, kissing me as we went. "Tour later, yeah?" he whispered between kisses.

"Definitely," I replied.

He led me to the stairs that led to the loft above and flipped the light on, flooding the room in a soft glow from the fixture above the bed, the very large bed. It was the prettiest thing I had ever seen, constructed of split logs and large enough for a small family. It rose up off the floor almost three feet and shone with the sheen of age and use. Trevor gave me a small push to get me further into the loft area. I looked over my shoulder at him and smiled.

****

~Trevor~

27

Trevor watched over Rebecca Ann's shoulder as the smile started to spread on her face. It was the only thing he could see at that moment. He slowly turned her in his arms and lowered his head, watching as her smile widened even more. It was a beacon, drawing him closer. The moment their lips touched, it was like coming home for him. It was everything he never thought he would have after what had happened to him with Janet. He knew that this was it, that Rebecca was his one. It was different than any other kiss he had experienced before. Trevor broke the kiss and said,

"Rebecca Ann, we don't have to do anything you don't want. This is for you. I just want to spend time with you, with or without our clothes on."

"Trevor, I don't know what I really want," she replied. "At this point, I am so conflicted. I definitely don't want Alan back, but I am not sure if I want to start a new relationship either."

"I get that," Trevor said. "I can wait. Let me get a pillow and blanket, and I will sleep in on the couch."

"No! I can't let you give up your bed," Rebecca practically yelled. "I'll sleep on the couch."

"Nope, sorry, babe. I want you in my bed, even if I'm not there," he replied.

"Fine, but you are staying in here with me then," Rebecca ordered. "I refuse to let you sleep on the couch. Besides, you're too tall for it anyway."
"You have a point, babe," Trevor chuckled. "Then I will sleep on top of the covers."

"I am gonna take a shower," Trevor told her. "You can do the same. I will use the guest bath, and you can use the shower in here."

"Okay, sounds good," she said. "Ummmm, do you have something I can sleep in?"

Trevor walked to his dresser and pulled open the third drawer down. He reached in and grabbed out a tee shirt for her to wear. Handing the shirt to Rebecca, he kissed her cheek and headed out the door. Rebecca heard a door down the hall open and then close.

Rebecca headed into the restroom and started the shower. While it warmed, she looked at herself in the mirror, looking to see what Trevor saw in her. She knew he wanted her, as she had felt his erection while they were making out like a couple of horny teenagers on their third date. All she could see was the woman that Alan had cheated on. A little overweight, long brown hair, and too large blue eyes. While she didn't think she was an ugly old hag, she didn't feel as if she was anything special. Rebecca shook her head and started to undress. What followed was the world's fastest shower. Once she was dry, she put Trevor's shirt on and headed out to the bedroom. Once there, she got into the bed to wait. It must have taken Trevor a while to finish up. She never felt him get into the bed, her eyes closing almost immediately in sleep.

Trevor entered his bedroom and stopped, looking at Rebecca Ann in his bed and wanting her to stay there for eternity. He couldn't reconcile that this beautiful, funny, and strong creature was chosen specifically for him by the Fates, as those bitches didn't like him that much. He was in awe. He settled onto the bed, staying above the covers just like he told Rebecca he would. He turned onto his side and watched her as she slept. She wiggled in her sleep, so he pulled her to him and continued to watch her. As she rested on him, he could hear a slight snore come from her. It was cute as fuck. Trevor hoped that this time he was reading the signs correctly; he would hate to be wrong for a second time. He wouldn't survive a second betrayal.

Trevor fell asleep thinking of how to tell Rebecca about his animal, his clan, and his disastrous time with Janet. That last one would take the most courage. It was a very dark time in his life. He was just glad that he had survived long enough to find Rebecca.

Chapter 2

~Rebecca~

Light glimmered through the drapes, waking Rebecca. She stretched and yawned into her hand. Turning, she saw Trevor sleeping peacefully beside her, still on top of the covers. She gave a small smile and wiggled off the bed, heading to the restroom to take care of her morning rituals. Once done, she started toward the stairs and to the kitchen below. Coffee, she needed coffee.

In the kitchen, she searched the cupboards and finally found coffee beans (an amazing Kona blend that was one of her favorites) and a bean grinder. She added enough beans for a full pot, pushed the top down on the grinder, and watched as the beans turned to an almost fine ground of manna before she added the beans and water to the coffee pot that was sitting next to the toaster on the countertop. While the

33

coffee brewed, she searched the fridge for something to make for breakfast. She may not be a raving beauty, but she could cook. She found eggs, bacon, and bread in the fridge and vanilla in the cupboard. French toast was one of her specialties. This was gonna be so good. She started mixing the eggs and milk with the vanilla and a little sugar. She felt strong arms wrap around her waist and then she heard,

"Babe, what are ya doing?" Trevor asked with gravel in his voice.

"Making you breakfast as a thank you for letting me stay last night," she replied. "I wasn't sure how to thank you for the inconvenience I'd caused. I'm sure you had better things to do than to babysit me last night."

"I would never have anything better to do while you're around, Rebecca Ann," Trevor told her, wincing. "I have some stuff to tell you."

"Trevor, you don't have to tell me anything, unless you want to," she said as she looked up into his concerned, stormy dark eyes.

"I want to tell you everything, babe," he stated. "Let's eat, then we can talk, yeah?"

"Sure," she said as she flipped the French toast. "Can you get coffee cups down and pour, please? I take three spoons of sugar and a little creamer or milk, whichever you have handy."

Trevor let Rebecca Ann go and turned to the cupboard above his coffee pot. Grabbing two large cups, he poured the coffee and added creamer and sugar to Rebecca Ann's, leaving his black.

"Yuck, how can you drink it straight?" she asked with a sour look on her face.

"I don't need any extras in my cup, babe. It puts hair on your chest," Trevor told her jokingly.

"So funny," Rebecca said. "You don't have a hairy chest, dude."

Trevor threw his head back and laughed. Pulling her to him, he kissed her, not hard and demanding, but soft and sweet. He could wake to this, to Rebecca in his kitchen, in his home, every damn day. He would need to talk with Marcus and the rest of the clan. They needed to know that he had finally found his true fated mate.

Rebecca broke their kiss and turned back to the counter. She picked up the two plates she had prepared and set them on the table.

"Let's eat," she said. "I have to get home soon. I have work this afternoon."

Trevor didn't want her to leave. He wanted to keep her in the compound with him and his clan. He didn't trust Alan at all, but he also wanted to keep Rebecca Ann to himself.

Once they were done eating, Trevor helped Rebecca clean up his kitchen. Rebecca was surprised and said as much. His reply that it was quicker with two surprised her, as Alan would have never helped with what he called "woman's work". Rebecca was just glad that she was finally free of him.

Trevor waited while Rebecca got ready to leave. While he was waiting, he went out onto his front porch. He saw Ian in the compound yard and called him over.

"Ian! Yo, Ian!" Trevor called.

Ian looked over and smiled as he headed across the compound to talk with Trevor.

"Hey man, what's up?" Ian asked.

"I need to tell you something," Trevor smiled widely.

37

"Dude, tone down the wattage. You're blinding me with those teeth," Ian joked. Then doing a double take, he asked, "Wait, why are you smiling?"

"I'm smiling because..." Trevor started to say, but then the front door opened to his cabin, and Rebecca walked out smiling shyly.

"Never mind, dude. I can see why you're smiling," Ian said.

"Ian, this is Rebecca. Rebecca, this is my best friend, Ian," Trevor introduced. "Ian, where's Lauren? I want her to meet Rebecca too."

Ian looked at Trevor in confusion. He hadn't introduced anyone to him or the rest of the clan since Janet. The shit show of that catastrophe lived on every day within the clan, like ripples on a lake that never quite calmed.

Trevor gave Ian a look to let him know he would tell him the whole story later. Trevor heard a door open across the yard, and looking behind him, he could see Lauren leading the twins towards their small group of three. Smiling, he waved. Lauren waved back, and then the twins yelled at seeing him and broke out into one of the most uncoordinated gallops he had ever seen. Watching them always made him laugh, and this time was no exception

"Hey, Lauren, I want you to meet someone," Trevor began. "This is Rebecca, and Rebecca, this Lauren, Ian's wife, and the two terrors attached to my legs are Noah and Liam, also known as the twins."

"Well, hello there, Noah, Liam. How are you?" Rebecca asked as she smiled down at the twin boys wrapped around Trevor's legs.

"Okay," Noah said. Being the more outspoken of the two boys, he always took the lead on any interactions with the grown ups. Liam preferred to run and play and shift whenever it was possible. Being only almost two had its disadvantages, as the boys couldn't quite control their shifts and sometimes they would tear right out of their clothes, leaving strips of torn fabric where ever they happened to shift at. While it was usually a natural occurrence, and no one would have to worry, they had not been as diligent as they should have on occasion. That sometimes led to quick exits from social events to the back seat of Ian's car.

Trevor watched the boys on his legs, playing and tugging on his pants. This is what he had always wanted: a mate and cubs of his own, a family. He looked up in time to see Rebecca Ann's wistful expression. He smiled a little brighter and grabbed her hand. As they tried to turn to go to the car, both boys started to fuss.

"That's my cue," stated Lauren, "that these little animals need breakfast."

"See you later, Lauren," Trevor called as he watched her pick up each boy and place them on opposite hips. He laughed as he heard the baby talk that Lauren was sharing with the boys. It was always good to see them all so happy after their near miss, when Lauren had been taken by Hatchet and his thugs.

"Alright, Trevor. See you later at the meeting with Marcus," Ian said, as he too turned to go into his cabin.

Trevor waved as he led her back towards his own home. He noticed she was shivering a little and said,

"Rebecca Ann, we'll take my truck into town. You're looking a little cold there, darling."

"Oh, well, we don't have to," Rebecca replied, "but it would be appreciated. If my mom sees me pull up on your devil machine, I'll never hear the end of it."

Trevor opened the passenger door on his 2016 Ford F150 he had purchased new a bit over six months ago. Midnight blue 4 x 4 with an ecoboost engine, it was one of the best vehicles he'd ever owned besides his old Indian that he and Marcus had restored when he was a rebellious teen. Rebecca settled herself into the seat and buckled her seat belt as she watched Trevor walk around the front bumper of the truck. She was still shocked that she had slept beside him. It just wasn't something she did. She didn't typically have sleepovers with men she had just met. Trevor opened the driver's side door and got into the truck. Closing his door, he looked over at Rebecca Ann, smiled, and buckled his own seat belt before starting the engine. As they travelled idly down the road out of the compound and back into town, Rebecca Ann and Trevor were lost in their own thoughts, each thinking of the other and what had happened. Rebecca was worrying that Trevor was just after a piece of ass; Trevor was worrying over how to tell her that he was an almost 700-pound polar bear and she was his fated mate.

Fifteen minutes later, they pulled into town. Trevor asked Rebecca for directions to her place. She directed him back towards the bar and said he could drop her there and she'd pick up her car and drive herself the rest of the way home. Trevor growled low and said,

"I'm not leaving you at the bar, babe. Forget that."

"But Trevor, I can make my way home," she argued.

"Nope, you are gonna show me where you live, babe," Trevor told her with authority. "I'm not leaving you out here, unprotected and alone."

Rebecca let out a sigh, "Fine, let's go then." She glared at Trevor and said, "Go left out of the parking lot, I'll direct you once we get closer."

"Rebecca Ann, don't look at me like that unless you want me to stop this truck on the side of the road.

43

I can get you to smile again." Trevor grinned, trying to get her out of her snit.

"I don't doubt that you can, Trevor," Rebecca replied, "but I want to be mad at you for a minute. You are acting crazy, and I can take care of myself."

"I'm sure you can darling, but why should you have to? I'm here and I want to take you home," Trevor said.

'Fine, take a left onto 43rd, and our house is the first one on the left," Rebecca grumbled.

"Babe, it'll be fine. You'll see," Trevor said.

"You don't know my mom. This is going to be a disaster," Rebecca sighed as she spoke, thinking to herself how she might get Trevor to just let her out at the end of her driveway. To say she had a complicated relationship with her mom was an understatement. Her mom, Lisa, was always

44

sunshine and rainbows around other people. Although she was a little handsy with the men Rebecca had dated in the past, and that worried Rebecca. She didn't want whatever this was with Trevor to end yet. While Rebecca was having her inner fight, they had arrived at her house. Trevor pulled the truck to a stop and went to get out. Rebecca reached for his arm and said,

"I've got it from here. Thank you for the ride. I'll see you at The Roadhouse."

"Babe, I'm getting out of the truck and walking you to the door. Then we will talk about seeing each other later, ok?" Trevor stated with a smile that didn't quite reach his eyes. There Rebecca saw a bit of worry and apprehension.

"Okay, let's go then," Rebecca said, resigned to the confrontation and humiliation that was about to happen. As she stepped from the truck, she heard a car pull up behind them. Looking back, she saw

Alan's car. Just what she needed to add to this already bizarre situation.

"Well, fuck," she muttered.

"Becca, please, can we talk?" Alan began.

"No, douchebag, you can't talk," Trevor growled out.

"I wasn't talking to you, Neanderthal," Alan said.

"Alright, boys, that is enough," Rebecca stated. "Alan, go home. I don't have anything to say to you. Trevor, let's get this over with. I need a nap."

Alan glared at Trevor. Trevor glared right back, while also making this really sexy sounding growly noise. Holy shit, he was sexy. She stared at Trevor, still not sure what this mountain of gorgeousness wanted from her, but she was hoping it wasn't just a one night stand.

Alan headed back to his car with a muttered, "Bitch." Trevor made to go after him, but she grabbed him by the arm. He stopped and looked down at her. He was pissed, his eyes almost glowing with his anger.

"Trevor, please let's just go in. He isn't worth it," she pleaded.

"You're right, he isn't worth it, but you are." Trevor replied. "I won't let anyone talk to you like that. Especially not that idiot."

She reached towards Trevor while going up on tip toe. She dragged his head down to hers and kissed him, hard. With tongue. No one had ever stood up for her against someone's cruelty. It was hot as hell. She deepened the kiss and rubbed against him like a cat in heat. Trevor pulled away, but she whimpered and tried to pull him back closer.

"Babe, we're in your front yard," he said, "and there is someone on the front porch."

"Rebecca Ann, stop being an exhibitionist and introduce me to your friend," Mom called from the top step.

She dropped her head to Trevor's chest and with a defeated sigh, stood straight and headed for the porch and her mother.

"Mom, this is a friend of mine, Trevor," she introduced, "Trevor, this is my mom, Lisa."

"Nice to meet you, ma'am," Trevor said. "I can see where Rebecca gets her looks from."

"Oh, why thank you, Trevor," Mom simpered. "It's nice to meet you too."

"Mom, really," she huffed.

"What? I'm just saying hello," Mom said with a smirk.

This was such crap. She needed to finally get back out of her house. Especially if Trevor and Rebecca Ann were to get to know each other better. Mom could be a force, like a category 4 hurricane. Nothing was safe in her path.

"Lisa, it was great to meet you," Trevor said. "Rebecca Ann, I have to get to work, but I'll pick you up later. Come back out to my place tonight. We have to talk, ok babe?"

"Sure, I get off work at ten o'clock tonight," she replied.

Trevor pulled her to him for a quick kiss, then he headed to his truck, started it, and pulled out with a honk of the horn.

49

Rebecca Ann watched him drive down the street with a grin. He was too good to be true, but for now, she'd take it. Rebecca and her mother both headed inside once his truck disappeared around the corner.

Chapter 3

~Rebecca~

"So, who's the guy?" Lisa asked

"I told you, that's Trevor," Rebecca replied. "We met at The Roadhouse and hit it off."

"So, what? You meet him and instantly decided to spread your legs?" her mom said. "Jesus, Rebecca, what is your problem? I told you they don't pay for it if you give it away."

And this right here was another reason Rebecca hated living at home. My mom was sweet and flirty around other people, but a raving bitch when it was just the two of them. That's how it had been since my daddy left when Rebecca was ten. I heard them arguing the night he stormed from the house. Money problems and my mom's flirting sent him into the night, never to be seen again. He always treated me like a princess. I missed him more all the time.

"Mom, don't be gross," I said to Lisa. "It's not like that. We're getting to know each other."

"Yeah, right. Is that what you kids are calling it these days?" Mom asked with a shake of her head and a sneer on her face. It was going to be a long day before Rebecca could escape to work.

"Mom, I'm going to shower and then take a nap. I have to be at work at one today," I said as I headed for my room to do just that.

I showered, thinking of my night with Trevor. I still couldn't believe I'd fallen into bed with a virtual stranger. I couldn't wait to see him later. I would love a repeat of last night's cuddle session, but today I find myself just missing his presence... I hadn't ever felt like a piece of myself was missing before. It was a disconcerting feeling. I shook off my thoughts and grabbed a towel. As I headed into my bedroom, I could hear my mom on the phone. I wasn't sure who she was talking to, but it sounded like whoever was on the other end of the line was angry. Mom was talking in placating tones, so she was probably talking to her newest loser boyfriend. I lay on my bed, and the next thing I knew, my alarm was going off. It was noon, time to get ready to go back to the bar. I loved my job, but I could do without the guys who thought it was my job to bring them beers and let them grab my ass.

I dressed for work and headed towards the front door to make the ten-minute walk. As I opened the front door, I yelled out to my mom "Bye, mom. I'll see you tomorrow sometime." Then I left.

I arrived at work with fifteen minutes to spare before my shift started. I went towards the back of the parking lot to get my coat from my car. As she got to the passenger side door, I looked down and saw that my car had a flat tire. Good thing Trevor insisted that I go with him the night before, because my spare was a flat pancake. I'd forgotten to take it to the local tire store last week to get a new one. I started a mental list of things that I needed to do tomorrow since it was my day off. I grabbed my coat and headed inside to start my shift.

I walked in the door and waved hello to Matt, the bartender on duty, and then got to work picking up my tray and heading for the tables in the main bar area. Orders came in steadily, helping to keep my mind off of a certain too tall gorgeous man.

Chapter 4

~Trevor~

I found myself thinking about Rebecca Ann all day. As I drove into town to pick her up, I knew I would need to tell her everything before too much longer. It was hard for me to keep my polar under control. All day, he had been pushing me to go into town and drag her home with me, where she belonged. I kept up a steady conversation with myself, trying to assure my animal that we would be with our mate soon and that I would tell her everything and we would be together. He hadn't been happy but by mid afternoon, he had stopped roaring in my head, which was a relief as I had another meeting with Marcus and Ian. There were still some hangers on from Hatchet's clan causing problems. Small things like graffiti on the wooden fence at the front of the compound, and things, mostly dead birds, thrown over the front walls, but the worst was the perimeter fences that were being cut. Someone or a group of someones was coming in the middle of the night and systematically destroying each side of the compound's fencing, cutting the fence and then running off like cowards. The first time it happened, I had been walking the property line just before dawn, obsessing about the fact that Janet had almost destroyed me, when I noticed a very large break in one of our fences. I thought a tree had come down onto the fence. Upon closer inspection, there was no tree, just freshly cut fencing haphazardly thrown to the ground. The second time it happened, we started nightly patrols. So far, that hasn't discouraged whomever was trying to sabotage and infiltrate our compound. Sometimes when the younger adults were in town, they would come back saying that they felt as if they were being watched, never actually seeing anyone. Just that eerie feeling where the hairs stand up on the back of your neck and you feel weirded out. This crap had to end. Once Hatchet was dead, we thought it would be over. Then when Janet disappeared, we were sure it was over. I didn't want this to touch Rebecca, so we had to get this under control and stop whoever was fucking with the clan still. I had to get to Rebecca. I was missing her like crazy and feeling more anxious by the second, now that the day was done. I hit the throttle of my old Indian and turned toward Fall City.

Once I was within the city limits, I eased back to just over the speed limit. No reason to be late picking up the most beautiful girl in the world because of a stupid traffic stop. I pulled to a stop at the front of The Roadhouse and cut the engine, unbuckling my helmet as I dismounted the bike. I placed my helmet on the seat and headed inside. I made it with plenty of time so that I could sit and watch my girl as she worked. I loved to watch her move. It was like poetry in motion, fluid like a river over small rocks.

I walked into the bar and sat near the back door. I watched as Rebecca Ann walked up to me at the table.

"Hey handsome, what can I get ya?" she asked with a smile.

"Your phone number would be nice, pretty girl," I replied.

She threw her head back and laughed. Not one of those dainty girly laughs, nope, not my Rebecca Ann. She let loose with one of the loudest, most joy filled laughs I had ever heard. It sounded like it was coming from deep within her soul. Her eyes were lit up brighter than the brightest star, and her smile was as big as Texas. I wanted to just pull her to me and... Fuck it, I thought on a growl as I stood and grabbed her to me. Drawing her closer, I lowered my mouth to hers and plundered her lips like a Viking returning from a successful raid at sea. I felt her mold herself to me and I deepened the kiss like it would be our last. We were joined at the lips, and I liked it. Slowing the kiss, I pulled away slightly. She followed and, on a small groan, reached for my neck. I took both of her hands and said, "Later, baby. I promise."

"Trevor, dang it," she mock growled at me. "Now I need to go change my panties."

"That's ok, darling," I grinned. "You won't need 'em in about an hour, anyway."

She giggled as she walked off to get my beer. I adjusted myself, my jeans digging into my erection so firmly I just knew I would have zipper teeth imprinted on my cock for days. I watched as she sashayed towards the bar. I smirked after her, not seeing that we were being watched from the far end of the room.

At a small table by the pool tables sat my ex, Janet, along with two other members of Hatchet's clan, silently watching and planning their revenge. I was oblivious, but I wouldn't be for very much longer. Janet was planning to make me pay, plotting to break me and the rest of my family, my clan.

I smiled at Rebecca as she made her way through the throng of patrons who were looking for a good time and a good drink before heading home to their lives. As she got closer, I could smell her need for me. I could see the want and the insecurity in her eyes. That shit needed to end, and end now. I was keeping her. As soon as I told her about my true self, she was mine. End of story.

"Trevor, lets go. I'm done for the night," Rebecca Ann softly said to me as she wrapped her arms around my waist in a tight hug.

"Okay, baby. I brought the bike," I said on a chuckle.

"The devil machine again!" she exclaimed on a giggle. "What am I gonna tell mama?"

"I don't know what you're gonna tell your mama, baby," Trevor said on a robust laugh, something that had been missing for far too long.

"Alright, let's hit it, big guy," she said. "I'm ready when you are. Just let me grab my coat from the bar."

She turned toward the bar to get her coat. As she moved away from me, I tugged her back and wrapped one arm around her shoulder, walking with her to get her coat, something I had never done with Janet. We left through the front door and headed to my bike, parked just to the right of the entrance. I handed Rebecca my smaller helmet that I kept hooked on the back of the bike and grabbed my own to buckle it on. I watched for a few seconds as she struggled with the chin strap, then with a laugh, I pushed her hands away and threaded the strap through the two metal loops and tightened it to her head. She smiled up at me with a Cheshire grin. I kissed her cheek and smacked her ass, saying, "Come on, babe, let's go."

"Trevor!" she squealed as she mounted the bike behind me, laughing and smacking my shoulder. I couldn't help but laugh with her. She had the power to make or break me. I was all in. No matter what was coming next, she was my everything.

I throttled the bike and hit the open road. As we left the lights of the town behind, I sped up and we took the turns toward the compound a little faster than normal, but we were perfectly safe. I had complete control, my human and bear senses working together to keep my mate safe. She tightened her arms around my waist as we took the last turn before the gate. I slowed the bike to ease us into the yard and came to a stop in front of my cabin. I could still hear Rebecca's giggle as we got off the bike. I clasped her hand and helped her unbuckle her helmet. Removing it gently from her head, I hooked it on the back of the bike and left my own hanging from the handgrips.

We walked up the two steps to my cabin door, hand in hand. I opened the door, and we walked through. Before I could close the door all the way, Rebecca was grabbing me and pulling me towards the loft stairs.

"Babe, we need to eat first," I said.

"Oh, I'm gonna eat all right," she replied. "Strip, babe."

I started to unbutton my jeans and pull my t-shirt from the waistband, but apparently, I wasn't moving fast enough, because Rebecca pushed my hands away from my zipper and took control. Lowering my zipper with a quick tug, she ran her hands up under my tee shirt, dragging the hem up and over my head. I had to bend down a little to accommodate her need to undress me, but I certainly didn't mind in the least. Before we could get all the way to the stairs, she had my pants to my knees and was working her way down to the floor. When her knees hit hardwood her hand pushing my pants down my legs had me stepping out of them when they hit my ankles and when she leaned into my erection, I about lost it. Feeling her warm breath that close to my crotch, I was suddenly like a teenage boy groping his first tit. I felt more than saw Rebecca take my ever rising head into her warm waiting mouth. She tongued her way to the base, taking small breaths as she inched her way down, licking and sucking like a kitten, mewling as she worshipped my cock. I looked down to see her bright eyes looking up into mine. It was one of the sexiest things I had ever seen or felt, and then she sucked, hollowing out her cheeks. She sucked again once more, using her tongue on the underside, and I groaned. I wouldn't last if she kept it up. Without thought, I dragged her up off her knees and fireman carried her to the loft, smacking her ass as I headed up the stairs.

At the top of the loft stairs, I set her on her feet and started to slowly remove her clothing as I walked her towards the bed. By the time we reached the edge of my bed, she was divested of all of her clothes. I lifted her up and kissed her deeply, once, twice and then a third time, before laying her on the bed and just staring, still not believing that she was my one and only, the one fate had chosen for me. I eased myself onto the bed at Rebecca's feet and slowly worked my way up her left leg with small love bites and quick swipes of my tongue. At her knee, I paused and worshipped for a long moment before continuing on my journey towards her core, where I could smell her want and feel her heat. Once I made it to her center, I licked once, twice, and then nibbled her clit. The whole while, she was moaning and gasping my name. Just what I liked to hear from her lips, my name and the moaning sound of her nearing release. As she began to crest, I applied just a touch more pressure with my tongue and added a slow moving finger to her inner muscles, and she came on a cry, that sounded like rushing water with my head gripped between her knees like a vise. She slowly relaxed her knees, and I made my way up, kissing a wet trail from her belly to her breast, stopping to fondle each one before covering her body with my own. I thrust into her core and almost came from the pulsating grip of her inner walls. She was still in the midst of her orgasm. I was in ecstasy. She was everything, and not just because we were so well matched in bed. I would have wanted her, even without ever having had her in a sexual way. That is just the way it is for us shifters, bears and wolves, tigers and lions. We all find our fated mate, and that is the end to our wandering ways.

I continued my thrusting assault to bring her to the brink again as I chased my own release, but I didn't want to finish without her cumming at least once more. It would always be about her when we were together like this or any other way, whether in bed or out. She always would come first.

"Trevor, Trevor, please more," she begged on a sigh. "I need more, babe."

"I'll give you all that you want, baby," I promised as I gave one final upward thrust, hitting her cervix and her g-spot with a small twist of my hips, finally giving her the second orgasm of the night that I had promised her as I too found my release. Sweat rolled off my forehead to drip on her bare breasts.

"Ohhhhh, yes!" Rebecca moaned on a loud exhale before going limp beneath me. With a small moan of satisfaction, I rolled to my side and pulled Rebecca Ann to me. She and I fit together perfectly, she was the little spoon to my big spoon.

"Rebecca Ann, I need to tell you some things...," I started to say when a loud banging on my door stopped any conversation. With a animalistic growl, I leapt from the bed and headed down the stairs to see who would dare disturb a polar bear with his mate. As I thundered down the stairs, I could see Ian out the window in my front door and I could hear him calling my name with panic in his voice.

I threw the door open to the sounds of bears fighting all across the compound's yard. Looking out, there were at least fifteen bears fighting amongst themselves and not all of them were our clanmates. I burst from my front steps and transformed into my bear, looking for a fight with whoever had dared attack us in the night like thieves. With a loud roar, I hit a large black bear I didn't recognize. I slammed

67

into him and slapped him with one of my giant paws, sending him flying twenty feet from where we had just been. On a rampage, I flew at him and slapped him a second time. This time, when he hit the ground, I went for the jugular. I was going to end this piece of crap who had dared infiltrate our home.

Before I could bite into his exposed neck, I heard whimpering behind me... I turned, still holding the unknown bear to the ground with my paws. I saw Rebecca Ann with a knife to her chest, pointed straight at her heart. Behind her was one of my worst fears come to life, Janet. She was back. Damn that woman. As a polar bear, I couldn't communicate, so I stepped away from the male black bear I had previously held to the ground. I made my way slowly towards Rebecca and Janet only to hear,

"Stop right there, Trevor, or the bitch dies slowly," Janet spit out.

I stopped and stared at Janet with what felt like fire lit eyes. I couldn't take my eyes from her. What was she doing here, and why now, when I had finally found my one? Not that I loved her still, not even close. The bitch needed to get over herself and under someone else, or dead. Dead would be good. I growled menacingly. I tried to keep my eyes on Janet, but they were pulled from her to Rebecca. She looked scared but unharmed, up to this point. She didn't even blink at me, even though I was an almost half ton polar bear. It didn't seem to bother her at all. I looked back to Janet, hoping she would tire of whatever game she was playing.

"This is what's gonna happen," Janet said. "Trevor, you're gonna forget this bitch ever existed."

I growled in denial, battling my bear to shift back to my human self so that I could confront my past.

"I don't think so, Janet," I replied. "You're gonna let her go and then you and your flunkies are leaving, or we'll end you all here and now."

"Oh, Trevor, you still think you're in charge," Janet purred. "Does this bitch fake it as well as I always did?"

Rebecca made a noise of disbelief, and I prayed she wouldn't say anything. I found that prayer would go unanswered when next I heard,

"Skank, let me go. I don't have to fake anything."

"Shut your whore mouth, bitch," Janet spewed venomously at Rebecca as she tightened her hold on her hair and placed the knife even closer to her chest.

"I've had just about enough of this shit," Rebecca Ann began and then heel kicked Janet and elbowed her the ribs. It was enough for Rebecca to surprise Janet and wiggle away from her. It was one of the most amazing things I had ever seen, a human woman getting one up on a she bear. As Rebecca ran from Janet, I shifted back to my bear and charged the bane of my life. Rebecca headed for the relative safety of my cabin. Janet shifted to her bear as I bore down on her. Roaring in my face, she lunged, missing me by inches. I slapped her down, but she got back up again. I slapped her down again. This time she lay there under my paw. The sounds of fighting died slowly around us. All of the intruders were in hand. Breathing hard, I waited for her to shift back to human. Once she completed her shift, I did the same. I looked into the face of a traitor and wondered what I had ever seen in her.

"Janet, this ends today," I stated. "We have been done for over two years. I don't know why you're here now, nor do I care."

"You'll lose this fight, asshole," Janet replied.

"There is no fight," I told her. "I have my fated mate, and it's time for you to move on."

"Move on?! Idiot, I can't just move on," Janet sputtered and screamed. "You'll pay for what you did to Hatchet, every last one of you!"

Janet struggled, trying to get out of my grasp. I didn't let up, holding her by her wrists to keep her away from my body. The one drawback to shifting was no clothes when we shift back to human. Very inconvenient.

"Regan, Valerie," I barked out, "get her out of my sight. I need to check on my mate."

I released Janet into their waiting hands and then

I ran for my cabin to find Rebecca Ann not cowering, nope, not my warrior woman. She was standing at the front window with my shotgun pointed outside toward the throng of mostly naked people.

"Rebecca, honey," I started, "let me have the gun now. It's over."

"Nope, not happening," she replied. "I'm gonna hold onto it for my own safety."

"Sweetheart, do you even know how to use a gun?" I asked

"Well, baby doll, I'm pretty sure you just point and shoot," she said sarcastically with a small grimace.

"Babe, I'm not gonna let anything else happen to you," I said. "Please give me the gun, ok?"

She lowered the shotgun and slowly extended it out to me. With a small cry, she let the gun go and lunged for me. I caught her up and hugged her tightly, whispering nonsensical meaningless words to her to calm her down. She was full blown crying by the time I sat us on the couch with her in my lap. I stroked her hair and back and whispered more words of encouragement into her ear, letting her know that she would be just fine and that I would protect her with my last breath.

"Baby, can you tell me how you ended up outside with Janet?" I asked her softly.

"I was inside, but I could hear the growls and roars and I got worried," she began, "so I got up and put your shirt on and headed to the front window. Once I got there and looked out, I was grabbed from behind." She was still crying jaggedly.

"Go ahead, get it all out," I said on an angry sigh. "I know this isn't your fault."

"You're damn right this isn't my fault, Trevor Mannus," she yelled at me. "This is that bitch's fault."

"I know, babe," I placated. "I know this is her fault. I need you to finish telling me what happened."

"Fine," she huffed at me.

I stroked her hair some more and snuggled her to my bare chest.

"I didn't know who had grabbed me," she started again, "but the next thing I knew, we were out the front door, and there were bears fighting everywhere."

I didn't know what to think about the fact that Rebecca wasn't more freaked out about the bears fighting in the front yard. I would think she would be shitting herself trying to get away from us, not cuddling into me for warmth and comfort.

"Trevor, are you listening to me?" She asked.

"Yeah, babe, I hear ya," I replied, somewhat distracted. Seeing her sitting on my lap in nothing than my tee shirt was getting to me. I could feel my eyes glaze over with lust. I inhaled and could still scent her fear and anger, but I could also scent her arousal.

"Trevor, let me finish this please," she half begged. "I didn't understand, but now I do. I knew about the people who could turn into bears. My granny used to tell me stories. But that's what I

75

thought they were, just stories, until tonight when I saw it with my own eyes."

I looked at her questioningly and asked, "Stories?"

"It's been a long time now, and granny's been gone since I was eight," Rebecca said.

"Ok, but what kind of stories, babe," I asked again. "It's important."

"Stories of people who could change from person to bear and back again and had one true love, a soul mate. And when they found each other, that was it... True love forever," Rebecca replied wistfully. "But those are just stories, Trevor. I mean, obviously the people turning into bears thing was true..."

"Rebecca," I interrupted as my thoughts turned over in my head, "I need to tell you so many things, and obviously you saw me turn into a polar bear. But you also need to know who that woman was."

"Not right now, Trevor, later," Rebecca Ann said as she leaned into me and kissed my lips lightly.

I took control of our kiss, deepening the contact and adding just enough tongue to make it interesting. I picked her up and had her straddle my hips while we stayed on the couch. Just as I worked my hand up to her left breast, there was banging on my front door. I stopped, lowered my head to her chest, and groaned. On a giggle, she pulled away from me. Sliding to the side of the couch, she let me up to answer the door.

"What?!" I snapped in to the face of our Alpha, Marcus.

"Sorry, Marcus," I said on a displeased sigh. "What's up?"

"Trevor, I need you and your friend to join us outside for a meeting," Marcus stated with a serious look in his eyes.

PA Vachon

"Ok, we will be right out. We both need more clothes on," I replied.

I closed the door and turned to find Rebecca heading for her clothes that we had left scattered on the floor of the lower level of my cabin from the night before. I watched as she dressed, entranced by her simple beauty. It was effortless. She didn't need to paint her face to enhance her natural good looks. She used cosmetics sparingly, as an afterthought more than a necessity. I smiled as she did that weird girl thing where they toss their hair around and run their fingers through it, looking freshly brushed without the brush.

"Trevor, you better get your clothes on," Rebecca chastised me. "Your friend, Marcus, sounded serious."

I snapped out of my voyeuristic pose and got into my own clothes. Once I was dressed, I took Rebecca Ann by the hand and led her to the main building

78

situated in the middle of the compound. We walked into a free-for-all yelling match. One side of the room wanted the traitors killed, the other side wanted them arrested by our shifter enforcers and taken into custody. Little did they know that they had three enforcers within their clan. We were a well guarded secret for a reason. Everyone saw us as the bounty hunters, when in actuality we were the hunters and on some occasions, the judge and jury depending on the crimes that were committed. I still didn't know how Ian kept it from his mate. Or if he even did, as it wasn't something we could freely talk about amongst even ourselves.

"Alright, that's enough," Marcus yelled to get everyone's attention. "We are here to decide what to do, not to fight among ourselves."

"I think it is obvious; they need to be given to the enforcers," one elder clan member said.

"No, they need to be ended now so that they can't do this again," another said from the other side of the room.

"Trevor, Ian and my fellow clan mates, what do you think we should do with the intruders? You've been quiet," he said.

"I think we should call the enforcers," Ian said, looking at Lauren grimly. He would always worry for his wife, especially after the kidnapping attempt from two years before.

"I agree," I seconded.

"Regan, what do you say?" Marcus asked his daughter.

"I think we should do whatever is best for the clan," she replied staring coldly at her father, clan leader Marcus.

"It is agreed then. We will call the enforcers at dawn," Marcus declared, and just like that, the meeting was over. I had held Rebecca's hand through the whole thing. I could feel her nerves, and the sweat was collecting between our palms. It was time to get her home. My home, where I could keep her safe and protected.

We headed back to my cabin and walked inside. No longer in a playful sexy mood, we sat together on the sofa side by side, each of us lost in our own thoughts.

Chapter 5

~Rebecca~

You would think that seeing your boyfriend... Man friend... Fuck buddy turn into a big ass polar bear would scare the shit out of someone. Not me, nope. I was that girl who used to listen to her granny tell stories of shifters and hope that they were real and that someday, a shifter would want me for his very own and carry me off away from my suck ass life. At this point, I'd take the occasional hook up because, damn, that boy sure knows what he's doing. I never thought orgasms could come in multiples, even when I was with B.O.B, my handy little vibrating friend. Sex wasn't the only thing on my troubled mind. I wondered who Janet was to Trevor. Was she someone I had to worry about? With my track record of picking cheaters, that would just about be the shit topper to my shit cake of a life. But I couldn't dwell on that thought process just now. I needed to talk with

Trevor. We had been interrupted trying to get freaky, when really we should have been talking.

"Trevor, I need to know.," I started to say when he held a hand up to stop my flow of words.

"I know we need to talk, and we will," he said. "I just can't wrap my head around what I need and what I want to say."

"Okay, we can talk later. Can you take me home please?" I asked.

"I can, but I don't want to," he said. "It's whatever you want, babe."

I didn't really want to go home, but I needed distance for the night. I was conflicted. On one hand, this giant polar bear of a man wanted me. On the other hand, he had a past that he was reluctant to speak about. I needed some alone time to think about what I really wanted. Not so I could make demands, but so that we could have a frank discussion on everything that had happened up to this point.

"Yes, take me home," I answered.

"Sure, let me get the keys to the truck, and we can go," he agreed easily. I had hoped he would put up more of a fight for me to stay, but I was glad he was being so easy going about it.

We got into the truck and drove in silence to my mom's house. Once in the driveway, I opened my door and turned to tell Trevor goodbye. The look in his eyes was so distant and cold. I hoped I hadn't ruined everything with asking to come home. I leaned over and kissed his cheek. He watched as I got out of the truck and walked to my front door. As soon as I opened the door, I heard his truck pull out of our driveway and head down the road. I guess this was it. I hoped to hear from him again, but I had my doubts. I walked into the house and headed for my room to think before I had to be back at work in the afternoon the next day. As I turned to close my door, I could see my mother watching me from the living room. It was going to be a long night.

I was just about asleep when I heard banging on the front door. I heard mom answer and then I heard the crash of breaking glass. I jumped from my bed and headed for the hallway to see what was going on. I opened my door and standing on the other side was the bane of my life.

"Alan, what the hell are you doing here? It's the middle of the night!" I asked.

"I need to talk to you, Becca, but you keep putting me off," he sneered at me. "I am here, and we are going to talk!"

"Fine, Alan. Let's talk," I said trying to humor him, all the while wondering where my mother was.

"Not here, we need to go," Alan said. "Come on. I know somewhere we can go to be alone so we can talk."

"Alan, I have to work tomorrow," I answered. "Can't we just talk here? I'll make us some coffee, okay?"

"We have to leave the house," Alan nervously replied, worried that the beefed up, nosy guy from before would show up and stop him from talking with her. "I promise I'll bring you back once we have a chance to talk."

"I don't really trust your promises, Alan," I said. "You promised you loved me and would never cheat, and look how well that turned out."

"What happened with Jerry was a mistake, babe," Alan said in a slightly raised voice. "I need you back; Jerry meant nothing."

"Whether Jerry meant anything to you or not, Alan," I said shakily, "I can't be with someone who can't be faithful. Jerry was my best friend, and I walked in on you guys playing hide the pickle in his ass, Alan. His ass! I don't care where you stick your dick anymore, but it definitely won't be in me."

I saw headlights pull into our driveway as I chastised Alan for his cheating. I wondered who could be here so late. We never had company this late at night. As I was about to tell Alan to take a hike, I heard Trevor calling my name through the screen door.

"Rebecca Ann, I need to talk to you, love," Trevor said. "I know I said I would give you space but I need you to come with me now."

I was happy that Trevor hadn't heeded my wishes. I needed him right now. I was glad that he was here to rescue me from sausage hiding Alan.

Chapter 6

~Trevor~

I watched as Rebecca Ann walked to the front door of her house and opened the door. Then I had to get out of there. So many things were swirling in my head that I didn't know which end was up or down. I couldn't believe Janet was back, and what the hell was she doing here? She had left the state and headed east, the last I had heard. I was confused, not about my feelings for Janet but for my need to keep Rebecca Ann close, and yet at the same time, I seemed to be pushing her away and keeping her at arm's length. I headed back to the compound, turning the thoughts over in my head and trying to make sense of it all. It was to no avail, as I was more confused than I had been before. I parked the truck once I reached the front of my cabin back at the compound and sat for a while, turning more of my past over in my head, back to the day that Lauren was taken and later that same day when Janet returned from wherever she had disappeared to before our fight with Hatchet.

Janet walked up to Trevor, and with a sneer, yelled, "How could you take the man who made me feel everything?"

"Janet, where have you been? I was so worried about you," Trevor said in confusion, not sure what was going on.

"Don't be a fool, Trevor. I was the spy on the inside for Hatchet," she said. "You and your clan took my soul, and now I'm here for some payback." Janet moved forward quickly, so quickly that I didn't immediately see the knife she held. By the time I saw the knife, all I could do was turn away, hoping to deflect the blow, but it was useless. I turned and the knife she plunged into my back came within millimeters of taking my life, but it did accomplish scarring my soul, leaving me bleeding, and killing my *hope a little more each day. As I lay bleeding, waiting for the end, my heart was breaking. I never thought that this would be how I would go out -- alone, a broken spirit of a man. I could hear the others making a grab for Janet, who had shifted and taken off at a run for the forest.*

I didn't see her again until today when she attacked my mate. My one true soul mate, whom I loved with every fiber of my being. She was my one and only. I loved her like a fat kid loves cake. I wanted her to be in my life, to be my mate forever, as long as we both had breath in our bodies. For as long as we both lived.

I finally got out to head inside after agonizing over my past and trying to incorporate my future. As I walked toward my front porch, I noticed a commotion off by the main building, so instead of going inside, I headed for the hubbub.

I reached the far side of the building just as an explosion ripped through the air, throwing debris up and raining down on the few of us that were standing next to the building. I looked at the damage and yelled out, "Marcus, Marcus, where are you?"

"I'm here, but I can't find Regan or Rory," he said in a panic. Rory was his almost two year old granddaughter. Regan would never say who her father was, although I definitely had my suspicions that I would never share. You could see the sadness in her eyes when she looked into Rory's startling green eyes. It was a look that showed pain, longing, and a touch of disbelief. No one was more surprised when she returned after being on a mission for the Enforcers with a much more rounded stomach than when she had left. She was well into her sixth month of pregnancy and not as open as she had been. We thought it had to do with Hatchet and his attempts at overthrowing Marcus and his plots to hurt Lauren. Little did we know that in the end, it would be so much more than that. I still wonder where Rory's father is after all this time and I wonder if he knows what he is missing by being gone.

I rushed to help look in the rubble of our main building, struggling to move the mortar, brick, and roofing materials that had fallen from the building when it exploded. I stopped after clearing a path to listen. I could hear a faint whimpering coming from the northeast corner of the building, farther away from the blast area. Although there were still many obstacles to get to the far side of the building, we all made quick work of the mess. Once we reached the rubble and tables that were overturned, I could still hear whimpering, only louder this time. I started to move tables and other remains out of the way. I got to one table that was still upright. Bending down and looking under the filthy cloth, I found Rory balled into her mother's side. Regan was not moving though, and her breathing was labored. I grabbed Rory up and handed her to the next person behind me so that I could reach Regan's side to check her over. I heard her moan in pain as I rolled her to her side. At least she was alive and could feel something, anything, even if it was pain. Pain was better than nothing, but the threat of paralysis was still not out of the question. I yelled behind me for the paramedics to be called. We needed to get both girls checked out as soon as possible. As the paramedics loaded the girls into the ambulance, I went looking for Ian and Marcus. I found them both on the other side of the destroyed building, arguing in loud tones.

"Hey, what's going on?" I asked.

"Janet and the others escaped during the explosion," Marcus sneered. "Our small building couldn't hold them, and someone here helped them escape with a diversion."

Ian looked off towards his house before saying,

"Lauren and the kids are fine, but I need to get back to them. Trevor, you should go and get your girl. There is no telling what Janet is capable of." Ian walked off towards his cabin, and I watched as the door was flung open and Lauren and the boys crowded around Ian and pulled him inside.

I left the compound after checking on Regan and Rory just before the ambulance left to pick Rebecca up at her mom's. On the way there, I turned over my past in my mind, wondering how to tell Rebecca about that disastrous time in my life. I knew I needed to tell her but I just didn't know how to start. Telling her about my polar bear the day before had been much easier.

Rebecca hadn't even blinked when my polar burst from my skin. I hadn't explained about fated mates, wanting to first tell her of my previous devious lover, but maybe I'd just call Janet my past girlfriend instead of lover. There was no reason to piss Rebecca off and make her mad at me so early in our relationship. There was plenty of time for that later when she was finally mine.

I pulled up to Lisa's house to see Rebecca talking to her ex. Alan, what a douche. I still couldn't believe that Alan had cheated on Rebecca and with her best friend, Jerry. I didn't like that she was outside. She should be inside, where it was safer and she was around people in case Janet should show up like she had the night before. I needed to tell her that she needed to stay inside. Next time she had to wait for me, or better yet, I'd leave a little earlier to pick her up.

I knew that Rebecca Ann wanted some time, but it was just too dangerous for her to be on her own. I needed her to understand that her safety would have to come first.

"Rebecca Ann, I need to talk to you love," I said. "I know I said I would give you some time, but you need to come with me now."

"Trevor. I told you I needed some space," she whispered as she wound her arms around me in a fierce hug. "But I'm glad you're here."

"I know babe, but I really need you to come with me," I said again as I held her to me. "Janet and the others got away, and I need to take you back to the compound. I don't trust her as far as I can throw her, which is pretty far."

Rebecca laughed at the image he brought to mind, despite being angry that she couldn't mull over the things that had occurred earlier in the day.

"Fine, let me deal with Alan, and we can go," she said. "But don't think this is me giving in. I'm still unhappy with you and I have a lot to think about."

Alan watched with curiosity and anger. Who did this guy think he was trying to take Becca from him? He was Alan Stein, and no one took what was his. Becca would come running back; he knew she would.

What happened with Jerry was a one time curiosity and wouldn't happen again, although it had been one of the best experiences of his sexual life. Jerry letting him dominate him by fucking his ass was a complete turn on. Becca would never let him have any ass time. But he could fix that if she would just be reasonable and listen to his apology.

"Alan, I'm done telling you that we're over," Rebecca said. "I don't want to have this discussion with you again. We're done, over, kaput. You need to leave me alone. I'm trying to start a new chapter in my life, and it definitely doesn't include your cheating ass."

"But, Becca-" Alan began.

"No, Alan, we are done. I have to go," Rebecca cut him off and headed for my truck.

Once in the truck, I looked over at Rebecca Ann, amazed that I had found my mate and that she was a sassy, sexy ball of contradictions. One moment she was insecure, the next she was flaying your skin with her quick words. What a woman.

"Trevor, let's go," she said. "I need sleep and a break from pushy men."

I could tell she was angry and not just at me. Alan must have said something that really set her off, and then I arrive to throw a wrench into her planned thinking time.

"Rebecca Ann, I'm sorry that I didn't give you more time and space," I said. "But Janet and the rest could really hurt you, and I can't risk that."

"Trevor, I'm tired of the bullshit," she replied. "Why do you care so much? We haven't even had a real conversation up to this point. We fucked, I don't know what we're doing."

All I could see was red but I wasn't angry at Rebecca. I was angry at myself for not telling her what she is to me. I was angry that Janet had made me so mistrustful that I couldn't be open with my one, the person who held my heart and soul in their hands.

"Rebecca Ann, I care because you are it for me," I said on an exasperated sigh. "You're my soulmate, the one person in the world that fate picked just for me. Because your granny was right. We turn into big ass, furry bears and have only one true love."

I looked over at the passenger side to see tears sliding down her beautiful cheeks. I reached across the distance between us and wiped one tear away. She turned her head and looked at me with her heart in her eyes.

"Trevor," she sighed, "Why would you say that to me? I'm no one's soulmate. I'm the girl everyone fucks over."

"Not me," I said. "I'm in this one hundred percent, you and me, babe. Forever."

99

Rebecca Ann huffed out a small laugh and shook her head, looking at me like I had grown an extra head. This was the reaction I had expected when she saw my polar bear, not when I told her that she was the end all, be all for me.

"I need to wrap my head around what you're saying," Rebecca Ann said. "I hoped you would want to date, have sex, whatever. I never thought you would say I was yours."

"Babe, you're mine, and I'm yours," I said. "That's how fated mates work for us shifters."

We drove on in silence, both contemplating the other's words. Each of amazed by the other's thought process but not sure what to say at this point. As I approached the compound, I saw a large car off to the left, bearing down on us at a fast rate of speed. I shouted a warning to Rebecca, hoping I would be able to outmaneuver the other vehicle. We were clipped in the ass end, close to the back tire of my truck. There was almost no damage, but we were pushed around. I looked into my rearview mirror to see David driving and Janet at his side. Before I could wonder what the hell he was doing back here, we were rear ended. The truck jarred, but didn't spin out. I accelerated, trying to get ahead of them enough to outrun the car, but my truck was no match for the smaller V8 keeping time with me.

"Trevor, I'm scared," Rebecca said. "What's going on?"

"Just some unfinished business, babe," I replied. "It'll be fine."

The car tried to rear end us again, and I turned my wheel just enough that he missed. I could see the compound just ahead, but the gate was closed tight and I hadn't had a chance to add the gate opener to my truck yet.

"Babe, do me a favor," I asked Rebecca. "Grab my phone and call Ian. His number is programmed in. Let him know that we are coming in fast and that we've got company."

Rebecca Ann grabbed my phone and did as I asked. I could hear Ian on the other end of the phone yelling at the others to open the fucking gate and be quick about it. I didn't want to hit the fence, but I would if it meant keeping Rebecca safe. Just before we reached the compound, the gate swung open and we sailed through. The car that had been chasing us stopped short of the gate when they saw the awaiting crowd of pissed off shifters, revving its engine they reversed and started down the road. I could see Janet yelling at David through the windshield. I couldn't hear the words, but I could tell they weren't pleasant.

I brought the truck to a stop at the front steps to my cabin. Rebecca and I both exited the cab at the same time, where Ian was waiting.

"What the fuck just happened, Trevor?" Ian yelled from his position near my front porch.

"I'm not sure," I answered. "I went to get Rebecca Ann, and on the way back in, we were hit by that car. David was driving, and Janet was in the passenger seat."

"David?" Marcus said in anger. "That idiot. What the hell is he doing back here?"

"I don't know, but we need to continue our twenty-four hour patrols," Ian replied. "I'm going back to the house to check on Lauren and the boys. Keep me posted."

Ian walked away at a fast clip. I knew he wanted to get back to his family. I knew the feelings he had churning in his guts. I felt the same way about Rebecca Ann. I had to keep her safe, no matter the cost.

I turned to Rebecca, who had been standing next to me taking in my conversation with Ian. She looked concerned. I took her by the hand and pulled her to my side as I led her to the front door of my cabin. I needed her in my house. I needed her to be with me, to be safe and protected.

I helped Rebecca to the front room and gently pushed her shoulder to get her to sit down and relax, although I wouldn't relax until Janet was gone from my life.

"Trevor, we need to talk about the fact that we're mates," Rebecca began.

"I know we do," I replied. "We also have to talk about Janet. You need to know what that's about."

And so, sitting there on the couch with Rebecca holding my hand, I told the story of how two years before, Janet was in on spying on our clan, how she reported our comings and goings that facilitated the kidnapping of Lauren, and finally, how she had attacked me once Hatchet was dead. I told how she stabbed me, and I bled. I bled a lot. Even as a shifter, I bled almost too much.

As I told my story, I could see the tears trailing down her cheeks.

She laid her head on my shoulder in a comforting way. I took my free hand and ran it down her hair. It felt like silk and was a soothing distraction. I settled back into the couch cushions, pulling her back with me. On a large sigh, I finished my story about how after Janet stabbed me, she shifted and ran. I told her how I hadn't seen Janet in two years. And that as soon as I met my mate, Janet came out of the woodwork like a long-lost relative looking to reconnect with a jackpot lottery winner.

Rebecca turned into my arms and wrapped her delicate hands up and over my shoulders, straddling my lap she cuddled in. It wasn't sexual; it was in an emotionally healing way. Of course, I still got an erection from the contact. She was my mate, so erections would happen until we were parted by death, hopefully a very long time from now after many happy years together.

I continued to smooth my hand over her hair, enjoying the silky feel of the strands, lulling me into a peaceful place. I slowly closed my eyes and listened to Rebecca's rhythmic breathing that signaled she had fallen asleep. I followed her into a dreamless contented slumber minutes later .

Chapter 7

~Rebecca~

I woke up and, with a stretch, realized we were still on the couch. We had both fallen asleep. At some point, Trevor had laid us down on the couch with me lying flat out on top of him. It was one of the most restful nights of sleep I had ever had. I looked up into Trevor's face to see him relaxed, almost with a smile on his face. I loved when he smiled. Since he didn't do it often, it always made me feel really special to bring out his happy. As I slowly extracted myself from Trevor's lap, I felt his arms tighten reflexively. I stilled, almost not breathing. I wanted Trevor to get more sleep. He was beginning to look a little haggard, and it worried me. Looking down at his face as I stood up, I had to admit it sometimes felt as if we had been together for years, instead of days. Literally it had been a couple days, not weeks, not years, just days. I was still blown away from the feelings that Trevor inspired in me -- the heat, passion, jealousy, and possessiveness that I had never felt with Alan. It was nice to feel wanted, needed. I watched him sleep for a few moments before heading for the restroom to shower and get ready for the day.

I started the water and let it heat up. As it came to temperature, I stripped down and got in. Just as I was about to close the curtain, I heard the door open behind me. Looking over my shoulder, I saw Trevor, his eyes glazed over a little, staring at my ass. I grinned at him and nodded my head in a 'come on in' kind of way. He smiled, stripped off his clothes, and headed right for me.

"Babe, you are the prettiest thing I've ever seen," Trevor said. "I can't wait to wrap you up in my arms."

"Trevor, you don't have to say those kinds of things to me," I replied. "I'm passable and I'm okay with that."

"Passable?" He questioned. "Baby, passable wouldn't give me a boner every time I saw you."

I smiled up at him and leaned into his large muscular body. On a sigh, I kissed his chest and twined my arms around his waist. I laid my head down and closed my eyes, letting the water hit me in the face. Luckily, I wasn't one of those people who hated water in their face or I would be making drowning noises right about now.

"Trevor, I want to stay like this for as long as you'll have me," I told him.

"Baby, that's gonna be forever," he stated. "I told you, fated mates are forever, till death do us part. Like when full humans marry, but we don't divorce."

I sighed again and looked up into eyes the color of storm clouds on a gray day. I smiled up at Trevor and worked my arms up around his shoulders. As I reached up, I pulled down a bit on him to get to his lips. Being just over five foot five to his six foot four was a little bit of a stretch when I wanted a kiss. As his lips touched mine, I rubbed against his erection, loving the feel of his silky hardness. It amazed me how something so hard could also feel so soft and warm. I let my right hand trace down Trevor's pectoral muscle and over his rock hard abs to the deep v that started at his hips until I had what I really wanted in my hand -- his rock hard cock. I gave him a gentle squeeze, causing him to inhale deeply. On his exhale, I stroked to the tip, applying just enough pressure to keep him on edge. On his next inhale, I stroked back to the base, to the nest of neatly trimmed dark curls. I let my hand then trail down to gently squeeze his balls. Upwards, stroke down and gently cup his sack, I then went back to stroking his dick, not too fast, not too hard. On my next downward stroke, I looked up coyly and slowly sank to me knees. Once on my knees, I stroked him twice more before putting my mouth on him, shallow at first and then a little deeper. I took him to the root. On the next upward slide, I used my tongue on the underside of his flesh. On the downward curve, I went a little deeper, taking him into the opening of my throat, at which point he groaned out my name in appreciation. I loved listening to him like this, knowing it was me and my actions that made him go weak in the knees. I worshipped at the apex of his legs for several minutes. I felt him take my head into his large, amazingly strong hands and start to slowly pump in and out of my mouth. I continued to use my tongue, adding in a little nip of my teeth here and there. Just a touch to let him know that even though he had me by the hair, I still was controlling this interaction. That lasted long enough for him to speed up and then stop. Once he stopped, he gave my hair a tug to get me up off the shower floor. I raised myself up and slowly kissed my way back up to his lips, stopping occasionally to drag my tongue over his sweat dampened skin. At some point, he had maneuvered his body to keep most of the spray from the shower head out of my face. We were kissing each other desperately, as if it would be the last time we would ever be intimate. Trevor pulled away from my kiss to look into my eyes, saying,

"Babe, we need to get out of the water. I want to fuck you in our bed."

"Our bed?" I queried as Trevor led me to the loft.

"Yeah, baby, our bed," he answered. "After finally telling you that we're fated to be together, there's no way in hell I'm letting you out of my sight again."

I sighed, partly in exasperation and a little bit lovestruck girl. I wanted to stay with him, but I was still afraid that I wouldn't be enough, that he would walk away or cheat like every other man I had been with.

"Baby, I see those wheels turning in your head," Trevor soberly said. "I'm in this for the long haul, no cheating. Ever."

"I know you say that, Trevor," I told him sadly, "but you can't guarantee that you won't stray."

"Not only do I guarantee it," Trevor said seriously, "but I also promise I can't cheat. Once we meet our fated mates, that's it. No more erection for anyone but the one that the fates picked for each of us."

I leaned into him and kissed him fiercely. I was so hot right now, one touch would set me off. And Trevor somehow knew it.

While I watched him, he trailed one of his large strong hands down over my hip and onto one ass cheek, pulling me into his erection once again. I wanted to climb this man like a freaking tree.

Trevor caressed my ass again, slowly working his way to my crack. One finger lightly traced my butt. He pulled me to him, using my long hair as a handhold. He deepened our kiss even more and walked me to the edge of the bed, caressing and kissing me the entire five feet from the loft stairs to the bed. As the bed hit the back of my knees, he pushed me gently back and worked his way to my breasts. Taking one

113

stiffened peak into his wet mouth, he took a sucking pull on my nipple, causing my back to arch up off the mattress. His other hand lightly twisted my right nipple and toyed with my breast intermittently. Once Trevor had my left nipple hard enough to cut glass, he moved to the right and proceeded to do the same thing. As he suckled at the my right breast and kneaded my left, I could feel his hard cock pulsate at my opening. With short jabs, he was dipping into my sex just enough to keep me on fire.

"Trevor, no teasing," I begged. "Please, I need you to fuck my needy pussy.

"Not yet, baby," Trevor said. "The teasing is half the fun."

"More like torture," I whined.

Trevor laughed. As I began to laugh with him, he slammed into me, deep. This caused me to gasp loudly in a mix of pleasure and pain. He immediately pulled almost all the way out, leaving my pussy gripping at his cock, trying to keep it deep inside. The feeling was like nothing before. On his next inward thrust, I could feel my orgasm build.

"Ah, Trevor...," I moaned out, "more, deeper... Please, babe, harder. I need it harder."

I was like a bitch in heat where his cock was concerned. The harder he fucked me, the better it was.

Trevor thrust into me a little faster and definitely deeper, hitting the opening to my cervix in a punishing thrust. The pain was welcome, not a hurting pain, more of a sexual pleasure pain. It was just enough to make sure I could feel him deep inside my pussy. I felt myself contracting around his invading dick. One thrust and then another, and I was orgasming harder than he had ever had me orgasm before. I opened my mouth on a silent scream.

Trevor followed me over the edge by milliseconds, calling my name hoarsely as he emptied his essence into my womb. Good thing for birth control. I was not ready for children, but I could see them later on down the road with Trevor's eyes.

Trevor, rested his head between my breasts, breathing heavily he said,

"Babe, I love you."

I was speechless. No one had said those three little words to me without adding 'too' after them. I had always said them first. After a moment, I was able to get him to lift his head. I looked deeply into his emotion filled eyes and said,

"Trevor, I will love you forever."

He leaned in and kissed me softly. I returned his sweet kiss with one of my own. I sighed contentedly and cuddled into his big form.

Trevor rolled us to our sides, dragging me closer to hold me tightly. I loved the feeling of security that his arms always gave me. It was like finally coming home.

Chapter 8

~Trevor~

I watched as Rebecca Ann slowly faded into an exhausted satisfied sleep. Once I was sure she wouldn't wake, I slipped from the bed to keep watch out my front windows. I was not going to let her be taken or hurt. She was now the most important person in my life. I would die for her if I had to.

As I stood at the window, I watched for any signs of trespassers and wondered when Janet would strike again. I also thought about Regan and Rory. I needed to ask Ian or Marcus how the girls were doing. Hopefully they would be coming home soon.

I watched the sun peek over the trees, a soft pink and red. I greeted the new day with a sense of unease. I could feel something coming but I wasn't sure what.

I was lost in thought and didn't hear when Rebecca Ann came down the stairs behind me. I felt her arms encircle my waist as she placed a kiss on my bare shoulder blade. I turned slightly to see her eyes. She smiled up at me with one of her high wattage smiles, the same smile that had drawn me in to begin with. This was the smile that made everything worth it.

"Hey, baby," I said. "Good morning. You want some breakfast?"

"I would literally sell my liver on the black market for some coffee right now," she replied huskily. Her voice was a mixture of sleepiness and roughened from our lovemaking the night before.

"I'll make some," I replied "Head for the table, and I'll get you your first cup of the day."

I walked towards the kitchen, watching her walk to the dinette table that I had in the breakfast nook area. Without an actual dining area, it was a great tucked away place to eat, drink coffee, and talk.

"Baby, were you serious last night about this being our place?" Rebecca Ann asked with uncertainty.

"Sweetness, not only did I mean it, I figure we can head for your mom's to get your things so we can get you settled in here," I told her seriously.

'I'll take you up on that," she said. "I was thinking for a bit before I came down. I want to be with you, Trevor. I love you and I don't want to be apart."

"Sounds like perfection, sweetness," I said with a grin. "You've just made me the second happiest man on earth."

"The second? Why not the first?" she asked with a silly grin.

"Because Lauren is pregnant again and that makes Ian the happiest man on earth," I replied as I sat next to her on the bench seat at the table that was set into the small nook off the kitchen.

"Aww, you're just a big ol' softy, aren't you?" Rebecca Ann smiled her cutest smile and leaned into me.

"Baby, I'm never soft around you," I teased. "As a matter of fact, I think we can wait to head to your mom's place." I snaked my arm around her waist and pulled her to me. Lowering my head, I captured her lips in a blistering kiss so hot it felt like fire.

"Trevor," she leaned away to talk, "if we're doing the whole moving in together thing, we need to head out and get my stuff. The sooner I am out of my mother's house, the better."

121

"Ok, babe," I agreed. "Let's get dressed and we can go."

We headed up the stairs to get the rest of our clothes. Once we were done, we wandered out into the compound to get into my truck. The weather was a little bi-polar in our part of the world, and it was pissing rain at the moment. Of course, we like to say 'If you don't like the weather, wait a minute... It'll change.'

We left the compound and headed into Fall City to Rebecca Ann's house. Pulling into her mom's driveway, I noticed a car that had out of state plates. It wasn't Alan, so I wondered who it might be.

"Babe, do you recognize that car?" I asked, concerned.

"No, I don't think so," she said warily.

I got out of the truck and headed around to open her door for her. I was concerned enough about the strange car that I wanted to keep her close to me. We walked up to the porch hand in hand. I was checking out the neighborhood, looking for any danger that may be present. My polar bear was on high alert.

Rebecca Ann squeezed my hand and smiled up at me in reassurance. I didn't let go of my vigilance, but I did smile back at her to let her know it was all good.

Rebecca opened the door and pulled me inside. Closing the door behind us, Rebecca headed for her room and I stayed near the door. I could hear voices coming from the kitchen area but couldn't make out the words. Unlike my animal, my human senses were normal. No hyper hearing or laser vision for me in my human form.

I looked down the hallway to see if Rebecca was on her way out when out of the corner of my eye, I saw Lisa in the kitchen with someone I was very familiar with, David. What the hell was he doing here?! Reacting purely on instinct, I headed into the kitchen at a fast pace, slamming into David I took him down to the ground. I could hear Lisa yelling at me, but my rage at finding an enemy so close to Rebecca drowned out her words. I smashed my fist into his face, the sound of cracking cartilage resounding off the walls of the enclosed kitchen. I drew my fist back to strike another blow but I was taken out by a frying pan to the head and I went down hard. I didn't lose consciousness, but I was seeing stars for sure. I reared back and let out a growl of frustration and pain. By this time, David had wiggled out from under my frame and was sitting up holding his nose, the blood running in rivulets down his face and onto his t-shirt. I heard Rebecca Ann come into the room and I turned to look at her to tell her to run to my truck and go. But instead, I watched as she aimed a double-barrel shotgun at David and then I heard I her ask,

"What the fuck is going on?" She seethed in anger. "Why are you guys beating each other up and who the hell are you?" she pointed the gun directly at David and stared.

"My name is Johnny Wallace," David answered nasally. "I'm here trying to stop Janet and the rest of Hatchets clan from doing anymore damage."

"Johnny?" I yelled. "Since when is your name Johnny, David?"

"It's always been Johnny," he said. "I've been undercover for the last three years, trying to stop Hatchet and now Janet from exposing us to the world at large."

"What the hell are you doing in this house?" Rebecca yelled at David. Or Johnny. Whatever the hell his name was.

"I'm here trying to warn your mother and you about what Janet has planned," he began.

"What the fuck is that psycho bitch planning?" I asked in anger.

"She is waiting until Rebecca is alone at the bar to take her and use her to trade for you and Ian," David said still holding his nose and speaking with a nasally tone. I smiled at the thought of the pain he must be in.

"And what about Regan?" I asked him seriously.

"That's none of your business," he said. "I'm just here to warn you guys to be vigilant in Rebecca's safety and then I'm gone."

"You can't leave, Regan needs you," I yelled. "She and Rory are in the hospital."

"Rory, who the hell is Rory?" he asked bewildered.

"Rory is Regan's daughter," I answered.

"Daughter?" he asked distractedly, "When did she have a cub? I mean, a baby?"

"Almost two years ago," I replied. "You didn't know? I know you two were close, so I thought you knew." I had discovered Regan and David's (Johnny's) relationship by accident. I walked up on them in the woods while I was out prowling in my polar bear form. Regan begged me to keep her secret, telling me she was ending it with him because she had discovered that he was part of Hatchet's band of miscreants. I didn't know why at the time, but it was making a lot more sense now. She broke it off that day, but I thought it was because he wouldn't leave Hatchet's clan. Now I knew it was to protect her cub.

Johnny closed his bright green eyes, as if in pain. I knew for sure Rory was his and Regan's cub now. I looked at him and said,

"You can't just leave. You need to go and talk with her."

127

He opened his eyes and said on a sigh, "I know."

I helped him up off the ground while at the same time telling Rebecca to put the shotgun away. I needed to find out more about what Janet was doing and why.

We all sat at the table, Lisa looking confused, Rebecca bouncing her knee in frustration, Johnny looking down at his clasped hands, and then there was me. I was sitting and taking in the room, looking at Lisa, Rebecca, Johnny, and then again at Rebecca before I started to speak.

"Johnny, I need to know what the hell Janet is doing," I said.

"She plans on taking out Marcus and all the others, including you. But definitely Ian. She hates him for killing Hatchet," he replied.

I sighed, wondering when Janet would be out of my life for good and when Hatchet's clan would stop with their antics. They were not thinking clearly, that's for sure, because if they were, they would know that any exposure of our secret other than to our mates was a death sentence waiting to be meted out by our Secret Keepers. I wasn't looking forward to upholding those judgments.

"Alright, this is what we need to do," I said as I began to outline a plan to stop Janet from hurting my mate. "Johnny, you'll go back and act natural, but keep me informed if Janet's plans change."

"What am I going to do, baby?" Rebecca Ann asked.

"You're going to take some time off work and spend time at the compound under guard," I said. "I need you to be protected."

"And what about my mom?" she asked.

129

"She'll have to come to the compound as well," I replied. That seemed to pull Lisa out of her fog.

"Thank you, but no. I'll be staying right here in my home," Lisa said.

"But...," I started to say

"Nope, I'm fine right here," she continued. "I have my shotgun and I have a friend or two that I can call to help me out."

"Mom, you need to come with us," Rebecca said at the same time as I said,

"I can't make you go with us, but call us if you need anything."

"I will." She promised.

"Let's go, babe," I said to Rebecca. "Johnny, call me if anything changes."

"I will," he said as he got up to leave. "Trevor, which hospital is Regan in?"

"She's at Snoqualmie Valley, Room 212," I answered him lightly.

"Thanks. I'll call if anything else comes up." Johnny said as he headed to the front door.

Rebecca and I stayed to try and talk her mom into going with us. I knew they had a strained relationship, but Lisa was still her mom. Lisa refused to go with us, so Rebecca gathered her things and we headed back to the compound. Arriving just a bit after dark, we took Rebecca's things inside my cabin and then walked over to the main meeting hall building to update Marcus and Ian on Janet's plans.

It didn't take us long to bring them both up to speed, and then Marcus headed back to the hospital to check on Regan and Rory. Ian headed to his cabin

to be with Lauren and the boys, and I took Rebecca
Ann home to our cabin.

Chapter 9

~Rebecca~

My mind was still reeling from the fact that Trevor's ex wanted to use me as bait. I worried for my mom; even though we had such a tumultuous relationship, she was still the only family I had left, and family was everything.

"Trevor, can we go to bed?" I asked in exhaustion. The late night before and the stress from today's discussions were taking their toll on me, and I just needed to rest. I also needed Trevor to wrap his arms around me and keep me safe.

"Of course we can, sweetness," Trevor replied. "Let's go get ready for bed."

Trevor let me use the facilities first, giving me some privacy. How he knew I needed it was beyond me, but I was grateful for the time alone. It gave me time to put things into perspective. I loved this man with everything that I was. I didn't think I would ever trust anyone again, but with Trevor it was easy; it was safe. I could be me, and he loved me anyway.

I finished in the restroom, then headed towards the loft where Trevor waited for me patiently. I crested the top step and saw Trevor sitting on the edge of the bed with nothing but his boxers on. What a sight! He was chiseled in all the right places. He looked up at me as my foot hit the floor of the loft and smiled. He cocked his head and looked at me.

"Baby, you're definitely wearing too many clothes," Trevor growled sexily. I could see his polar bear flashing in his eyes, stormy gray to a light golden hue and back again. I shivered in anticipation, walking slowly over to where he sat. I stepped between his slightly spread legs and looked into his eyes. He gazed up at me with love and adoration, something I wasn't used to seeing in someone's eyes when they looked at me.

"What's that thought, baby?" he asked as I bit my lower lip.

"I'm just amazed that you want me," I answered him honestly. "I'm not sure what to do with all the feelings that you evoke."

"You and me both, sweetness," he said, reaching up as he pulled me tighter to him, hugging me close. I felt his hands rubbing in circles on my back as he breathed in my scent, burying his head into my abdomen. I ran my hands through his hair lightly, trying to give him some measure of comfort and let him know I was there for him. Whatever he needed, I would give. He looked up at me then and pushed me back a bit. Standing up, he pulled me back to his body. Kissing me deeply, I moaned in pleasure, loving the feeling of his tongue, the nibbling of his teeth on my lower lip. I wound my arms up and around his shoulders, going up on tiptoe to get closer

135

to him. Trevor trailed his hands down to my ass, caressing me softly. He then picked me up like I weighed nothing, pulling me up his body. With an eep of surprise, I wrapped my legs around his torso and held on for dear life.

Trevor turned us around so that my back was facing the bed. Lowering me slowly, he covered me with his large hard body, slowly rubbing his erection between my legs, giving me just enough pressure from his hardness to make me squirm around trying to get more contact. I loved when he teased me, but right then was no time for teasing. I growled in frustration, and Trevor broke our kiss to look down at me and asked,

"What's wrong, baby?"

"Wrong? Nothing's wrong," I replied. "I just need you naked and inside my pussy before I explode from need."

"Whatever you say, babe," Trevor huffed out a laugh as he moved off me. I watched as he lifted his hands to the waistband of my barely there panties. He took one side into his hands and ripped the side seam. He did the same with the other side. I gasped at the sound of the tearing material.

"Trevor!" I yelled. "Those were my favorite panties."

"That's ok, Rebecca Ann," he replied, as he removed his own underwear. "I'll buy you new ones later."

I was not amused, but soon enough I forgot my tiff and lost myself in the pleasure of Trevor's touch. Just when I thought I couldn't take anymore teasing, Trevor thrust up into my wet heat. I moaned out his name as he began to hammer into me. It was rough, animalistic, and a little crazy, but I loved every moment. By the fifth thrust, I was there and couldn't wait any longer.

137

"Trevor, I'm gonna cum," I gasped out in bliss.

"Not yet, baby," he replied, winded. "Almost there, sweetness. Almost."

I crested the peak moments before I felt Trevor's cock spasm. I felt his pleasure hitting my womb opening like a rocket. I hadn't ever felt a man's cum hitting my womb before, and when I did, it made me cum again. My pussy tightened on his spasming cock, and we both moaned out.

Trevor rolled to the side and dragged me halfway over his body, running his right hand through my hair and gasping for air. I smiled into his shoulder, loving the thought that I had made this big handsome man cum. It was like skydiving without a parachute -- exhilarating and frightening all at once. I snuggled up and closed my eyes.

We were only asleep for a matter of minutes when the sound of the front door splintering open woke us both. Yelling could be heard outside. Trevor jumped from the bed, shifting before his feet even hit the floor. I watched as his polar bear slammed into the dark clothed figure at the top of the stairs. I heard them both hit the living room floor with a loud crash. I grabbed my shirt and ran to the side rail of the loft to see what was happening. I watched as the uninvited guest morphed into a bear as Trevor's polar bear took another pass at the intruder.

I watched as Trevor and the unknown bear tumbled around trying to bite each other. In horror, I saw the other bear bite into Trevor's snowy white fur, which then bloomed red. With a load roaring growl, Trevor grasped the other bear by the throat and bit down, and the crunching of neck bones could be heard upstairs. On a whimper, the smaller bear went limp and shimmered into a very naked Janet. Her breathing was ragged. She struggled to get up. One last attempt, and she breathed her last. Trevor looked up at me, still in his bear form, with a kind of sadness in his eyes. I knew he didn't love her anymore, but I could feel that he hadn't wanted to kill her either. Trevor shifted, backing away from Janet's body. He looked up at me again as I started down the stairs, grabbing a long tee shirt on the way down. I ran to him, jumping into his arms and checking him for wounds simultaneously.

"Trevor, are you ok?" I asked. "Where are you hurt?"

"I have some small punctures on my arms and the back of my neck," he replied, "but they'll heal relatively quickly."

"Not quickly enough," I huffed at him.

"I'll be just fine," Trevor said while holding me closer. "I need to get outside and see if everyone is alright."

"I know, babe," I said. "I'm going with you."

Before we headed outside Trevor put on his pants, leaving the top button undone and I grabbed my yoga pants from earlier in the day.

We walked outside, hand in hand, and looked at the destruction around us. Broken windows, wrecked cars, destroyed fences. The front gate was hanging at an odd angle, caused by the car that had blasted through it. It was a war zone. Hopefully, now it was over

Marcus walked up to us and said, "We've neutralized the rest of them. Where's Janet?"

"Gone, she's gone," Trevor answered. "I didn't have any other choice she was here for Rebecca."

"I know, son," Marcus said, giving his shoulder a manly pat. "Sometimes we have to do things we don't want to in order to protect the ones we love."

There was a story there, I could tell, although it was none of my business. I would wonder about it from time to time, I'm sure, but I would never ask Marcus to tell me his story. I was a little scared of the large grizzly clan leader.

"I need to get Janet out of the cabin," Trevor said. "I can't go back inside until her body is gone."

"Don't worry about it," Marcus said. "While we've been talking, Ian and some of the others removed the body."

"Thank you," Trevor said respectfully.

I took Trevor's hand and led him toward the cabin. I knew that he would need me to be strong for him. I could feel it in my bones. It was like a sixth sense, knowing that my strength would help him to heal. Once inside, I closed the splintered door as best as I could and led Trevor back up the stairs to our bed. I helped him out of his clothes and into the bed then I removed my own and lay beside him, holding him and quietly murmuring nonsense to help him to relax.

Trevor pulled me even closer. He kissed me softly, almost reverently. I stopped muttering to participate in the most loving kiss I had ever received.

"Babe, I need you," Trevor said. "I need to claim you so my bear will stop the constant roaring in my head. He's going just a lillle crazy."

"I need you too," I replied. "I accept all of you. Human and bear, I love you both."

Trevor pulled me across his body and began to run his hands up and down my back, stopping just before my ass to work his hands back to my shoulders. I started a slow grind on his growing erection, trying to get more friction between us. I loved feeling him get harder by the second. Trevor was a shower, but he was also a grower. His length and girth were almost too much to bear with me on top. The pain from his cock entering me added to the pleasure I was feeling at the same time. As we moved together, I could feel my orgasm racing to the surface. I groaned in frustration, not wanting to get off too soon and leave Trevor wanting. He slowed my movements with his large hands at my hips. He rolled us, slowly thrusting into me. I arched from the bed in pleasure, wanting more I began to move faster trying to get to that precipice of pleasure.

"Trevor, please make me your one," I begged between moans.

"You were always my one," he replied. "Now I'm going to claim you forever."

Trevor pulled me closer and kissed the heartbeat at my throat, opening his mouth to place hot, wet kisses along my neck I felt his teeth puncture my flesh. I felt a slight pinching pain as he claimed me as his mate and then all I felt was the searing pleasure as we became one.

I could feel his emotions coursing through me, just as I could tell that he could feel mine from the look of awe in his stormcloud eyes. His love for me was overwhelming. I felt tears well in my eyes and leak down my cheeks.

"Rebecca Ann, why are you crying?" Trevor asked in confusion.

"Because, I'm finally happy, Trevor," I replied. "Truly happy."

"Me too, baby," he said. "Me too."

Epilogue

Four weeks later

Trevor watched as Regan walked away from Johnny for the umpteenth time. It was starting to be embarrassing how many times the poor guy tried to talk to her. Trevor looked over to see Rebecca Ann and Lauren talking and watching the twins.

No one knew yet, but his Rebecca Ann had told him just this morning that they were going to have a cub. The birth control she was on no match for his seed. He was the happiest he'd been since the day he and Rebecca had mated.

A cub. Was he ready? He hoped he lived up to what Rebecca saw in him. She had returned to work the day before. Not alone. Trevor sat at 'their' table and watched her throughout her shift. No one gave her a hard time or made inappropriate advances while he watched from the side of the bar area.

She laughed at something Lauren said and the smile on her face called to him. He walked over and slung his arm around her shoulders, smiling into her eyes when she looked up at him.

"If I didn't know better," Lauren said, "I'd swear you two had a secret."

Laughing, I replied, "No secret, we're just happy."

"Uh huh, sure," she jokingly said, glancing over to where Ian was. I watched as she slowly rubbed her growing belly. I couldn't wait until Rebecca started to show. I knew I would be just as devoted to her as Ian was to Lauren and the twins.

Life was good. It could only get better from here.

Alone in the distance, a woman watches. Is she friend or foe?

Note from the author…

Thank you for continuing on this journey with me. You can connect with me on facebook

www.facebook.com/pa.vachonauthor.33

on my website

www.sexyshifterromance.com

and on twitter

www.twitter.com/PAVachonauthor

You can also sign up for my monthly newsletter on my website.

Keep reading for a sneak peek as well as a cover reveal for book three in the Bears in Love series...Bearly Mistaken, the story of Regan, Johnny, and their cub Rory. Smooches!

Bearly Mistaken

Bears in Love Book 3

Releasing March 2018

Winter 2015

Regan knew in her heart that she would do whatever it took to protect the unborn cub in her womb. I was going to be a mom. It wasn't ever one of the things I'd dreamed of as a child. My own mother had passed away the year before Trevor had joined the clan. I had just turned eleven that year. I had missed all of the mother-daughter milestones. Instead, I'd had my dad, Marcus, who loved me and cared for me, but when it came to girl things, he was clueless. Those were some rough years. Luckily, one of the older female members of the clan had taken me into town when I needed a bra, when that dreaded time of the month had started, and again when I was old enough to start thinking about sex because condoms were a must... No baby for the teenage princess of my clan. Condoms and unplanned pregnancy weren't important once you found your mate, though. My dad was going to shit a brick when he found out he was going to be a grandpa. I was an unmated twenty year old princess now. This was craptastic.

Regan watched as David made his way to their spot, a small pond just up the road from the family compound covered in a light dusting of snow at this time of year. It was such a peaceful place, lush and green in the spring and summer. It was the perfect place to spend time with your mate, even if he refused to claim you. The lush grass was a wonderful place for an afternoon of lovemaking. That's what it was, lovemaking. We weren't fucking or just having sex... We loved each other. Or at least, I loved David and I thought he loved me. But you can't always have everything that you want. Sometimes life gets in the way. The upcoming conversation was not going to be pleasant, but it was something that we had to talk about. David still didn't know about the life I was growing inside of me, our little miracle. Our cub. So far I had been able to hide it from everyone. I didn't have much more of that time left though. I still hadn't told David about the fact that I was one of the Secret Keepers, the enforcers for the shifter community. The enforcers and our clan of grizzlies had been fighting with Hatchet, a maniac leader of a clan of black bears that were too close to exposing our secrets. We were sometimes judge, jury, and executioner in certain situations.

"Babe," David smiled at me, "I'm glad you're here. We need to talk."

"I know we do," I sighed heavily, not really prepared for our upcoming discussion.

"Regan, it will be fine," he replied. "You'll see."

"It won't be though," I murmured.

"I know you think that it won't," David said. "But I promise you, we'll be together soon."

"We can't be together if you won't leave that psychotic clan of bears," I said as I raised my voice in frustration. This wasn't the first time we'd had this particular discussion.

153

"Regan, you have to trust me," David said.

"David, you're my mate, and I trust you," I said, "but mate or not, I can't break our laws."

"I know, baby," David sighed out in defeat, "but I have to stay and see this through."

"You don't have to be part of a rogue clan," I replied. "I'll talk to my father. He'll let you join us. Especially since we are mates. He would never make us stay apart."

"I just can't," David said again.

I looked at David sadly, not understanding why he insisted on being a part of Hatchet's clan. It was insanity. Those bears were going to get our species discovered. No matter what I said, he refused, and I wouldn't tell him about the cub just to get my way. I couldn't manipulate him in that way. He needed to want to stay for me, not just because a small life was joining our world in just over six months. We were both shifters, so the pregnancy would be more like a grizzly than a human.

"David, I need you to join me with my father," I begged, and I didn't typically beg. "I can't be with you if you're going against our most sacred of laws."

"I'm sorry, Regan," David replied. "I can't leave them."

"Then I can't do this with you anymore," I said as I cried silently, tears leaving wet tracks on my face, dripping off of my chin.

I turned away to leave, walking quickly back to my small Honda. I got in the driver's seat, wiped my eyes, and started the car. The engine came to life with a small growl, like a squirrel protecting its horde. As I drove away, I turned on the radio, and much to my chagrin, Sara Evans 'A Little Bit Stronger' was just starting, one the best anthems for heartbroken strong women everywhere. I sang along as I let the tears

155

flow, knowing that this was it. No mate, no love, just a product of our time together quickly becoming a reality.

I pulled into the compound and turned off the engine, wiping my face one last time before I got out of my car and started to walk towards my father, Marcus, to let him know about his grandchild. Instead I was sent out on an emergency enforcer mission that would keep me away from home for almost my entire pregnancy.

Made in the USA
Columbia, SC
26 September 2023